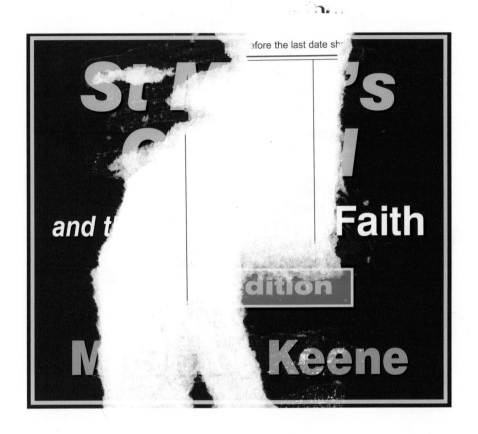

St ...'s
... ...
and t... Faith
...dition

M... Keene

 Nelson Thornes
a Wolters Kluwer business

First published in 1999 by:

Stanley Thornes (Publishers) Ltd

Second edition published in 2002 by:

Nelson Thornes Ltd
Delta Place
27 Bath Road
CHELTENHAM
GL53 7TH
United Kingdom

06 07 08 09 / 10 9 8 7 6 5 4 3 2

A catalogue record for this book is available from the British Library

First edition: ISBN 0 7487 4309 X

Second edition: ISBN 0 7487 6775 4

Edited by Kim Richardson

Illustrations by Angela Lumley and Steve Ballinger

Designed by eMC Design

Printed and bound in China by Midas Printing International Ltd.

Acknowledgements

With thanks to the following for permission to reproduce photographs and other copyright material in this book:

Andes Press Agency / Carlos Reyes-Manzo, pp 13, 31, 68; Corel (NT), pp 61, 107; PPL / Gordon Frickers, p 27; Sonia Halliday, p 17; Trip / F Good, p 12. All other photographs by The Walking Camera.

Scriptures quoted from the *Good News Bible* published by The Bible Societies/HarperCollins Publishers Ltd., UK, © American Bible Society, 1966, 1971, 1976, 1992.

Every effort has been made to contact copyright holders and we apologise if any have been inadvertently overlooked.

Contents

Key Question

What do we know about the Romans and the Jews who controlled the country into which Jesus was born?

Israel (Palestine) was a long, narrow country in the eastern Mediterranean; in area it was much the same size as Wales. The river Jordan bisected the region (see map) from top to bottom, running through a great crack in the earth's surface which formed the lowest depression on earth. At its northern end the river ran through the Lake (or Sea) of Galilee, a freshwater lake 230 m below sea-level, before dropping a further 180 m to reach the Dead Sea. The Lake of Galilee was also known as the Sea of Tiberias.

As you will see from the map, the River Jordan meandered considerably on its journey. It was just 120 km from the Lake of Galilee to the Dead Sea as the crow flies, but the river travelled more than twice that distance. True to its name, the very high saline content of the Dead Sea, an inland sea without an outlet, prevented any vegetation from growing on its banks – or far beyond. The area was so hot (the temperature was over 40°C in the summer) that as much water evaporated from the Dead Sea as flowed into it from the River Jordan.

The River Jordan, bisecting the land of Israel, had a great effect on the everyday lives of the people who lived there.

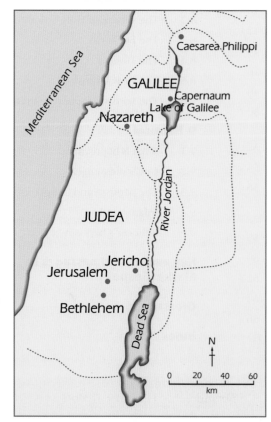

The Romans

The Romans conquered Palestine in 63 BCE and appointed Herod the Great, a half-Jew, to govern it for them from 37 BCE. Herod was tolerated by the Romans because he was prepared to put their policies into action ruthlessly in his area. The much-hated Herod was king when Jesus was born in Bethlehem around 5 BCE, but when Herod died shortly afterwards, the Romans divided his kingdom up between his three sons. One of them, Archelaus, was so cruel that the Romans soon replaced him with a governor (procurator) of their own, a post to which Pontius Pilate was appointed in 26 CE. He stayed in his position for ten years before being replaced by the Romans, again for excessive cruelty.

The Romans allowed the Jewish inhabitants of Palestine to have their own Council (the Sanhedrin) which was made up of 71 priests (mainly Sadducees), Pharisees and other Jewish leaders under the chairmanship of the High Priest. The Sanhedrin always met in Jerusalem; it had the authority to pass laws on religious matters, to punish those who broke the religious laws and to help the Roman authorities to maintain law and order in Palestine. Both the Sanhedrin and Pontius Pilate played an important role in securing the death of Jesus in 29/30 CE. You will find out much more about this in Unit 3.

The Jews

The Jewish faith was, and remains, unique. This faith in the one God (called 'monotheism') who had made a special covenant (agreement) with the Jews was shared by Jesus and most of his early followers. It was based on three pillars:

1 The Torah (the teaching). The Jewish Scriptures were made up of three parts – the Torah, the Prophets and the Writings. Of these the Torah was the most important. The Torah, the first five books of the Jewish Scriptures (Genesis, Exodus, Leviticus, Deuteronomy and Numbers), told how God had revealed his laws to Moses at Mount Sinai after the Jews had left their long slavery in Egypt. The Ten Commandments stood at

the heart of the Torah, although the Jews were given 613 laws altogether by God to keep. Orthodox Jews today still try to keep these laws as conscientiously as they can.

2 The Temple. The first Temple had been built in Jerusalem by King Solomon in the 10th century BCE. It was destroyed by the Babylonians in 586 BCE and then later rebuilt by Herod the Great. In the time of Jesus, the Jews, who were dispersed throughout the Roman Empire, made every effort to reach the Temple for the great religious festivals each year – especially Pesach (Passover). The Temple was finally destroyed by the Romans in 70 CE, forty years after the death of Jesus, following a Jewish revolt. It was never rebuilt.

3 The Synagogue. No one knows when the first synagogue ('a place for coming together') was built, but synagogues meant that people no longer had to travel to the Temple in Jerusalem to worship God. Instead, Jews could meet in their local synagogue for prayer and study. Jews today still come together in synagogues for the same reasons.

Religious groups

The most important religious group at the time of Jesus was the Pharisees ('the separated ones') who frequently came into conflict with him in Mark's Gospel. They tried to keep the Torah pure by surrounding it with many extra laws of their own – especially over keeping the Sabbath day (Shabbat). The Sadducees were wealthy land-owners, priests in the Temple and friendly towards the Romans. By contrast, the Zealots ('dagger-carriers') were a small, revolutionary group violently opposed to anything Roman. Jesus chose a Zealot, Simon, as one of his disciples. Judas Iscariot, who betrayed him, may have been a Zealot as well.

Key Points

1 The land of Israel fell under Roman domination in the 1st century BCE and Herod the Great was appointed to govern it for them. In the time of Jesus Pontius Pilate was the Roman procurator or governor.
2 The Romans allowed the Jews to have their own council, the Sanhedrin.
3 Jewish faith was based on the three 'pillars' of the Torah, the Temple and the synagogue.
4 The Pharisees were the most important Jewish religious group. The Sadducees and the Zealots were also influential.

Work to do

1 a What were the three foundations on which the faith of the Jewish people were built?
   b What do Jewish people mean when they speak of the 'Torah'?
   c How was the Torah first given to the Jews?
   d Why is the Torah so important to the Jewish people?
2 Write short notes on:
   a the Pharisees
   b the Sadducees
   c the Zealots
   d the Temple
   e the synagogue
   f the Sanhedrin.

In the Glossary

Gospel • Herod the Great • High Priest • Jerusalem • Judas Iscariot • Moses • Pesach • Pharisees • Pontius Pilate • Sabbath day • Sadducees • Sanhedrin • Synagogue • Temple • Ten Commandments • Torah • Zealots

1.2 Mark and his Gospel

Key Question

Why did Mark write his Gospel and where did his information come from?

Jesus was crucified by the Romans in Jerusalem around 29 CE, yet Mark did not write the first Gospel (a word meaning 'Good News') in the New Testament until almost 40 years later. In the meantime recollections of Jesus were shared by Christian believers as they met together by word of mouth (a process known to scholars as 'oral transmission'), and this kept the memory of Jesus very much alive in the early Church. There was no great urgency to write these recollections down since the early Christians were convinced that Jesus would come back to the world during their lifetime, as he had promised to do. Mark clearly shared this belief, since he quoted Jesus as saying:

> "I tell you, there are some here who will not die until they have seen the Kingdom of God come with power."
> (9.1)

Mark's Gospel

Mark wrote his Gospel around 65 CE. By this time he had come to the firm conclusion, as had many other believers, that Jesus was not going to return in the foreseeable future.

Mark did not refer to either the birth or the childhood of Jesus in his Gospel. He started his account of the life and teaching of Jesus with the work of John the Baptist.

Mark was also spurred on to write by the persecution which Nero, the Roman emperor, had brought on the Church in 64 CE, during which many Christian leaders, including Peter and Paul, died. Such leaders as these were the main source of information to other Christians about Jesus. Now that they were dying without warning there was a danger that this invaluable information about Jesus would die with them. To confuse matters further, new converts were flooding into the Church, most of whom came from a pagan background with little knowledge of the Jewish Scriptures. A written record of the life and teaching of Jesus was desperately needed.

In his Gospel, Mark told his readers that his book was about the Good News (the Gospel) of Jesus Christ, the Son of God. Mark alone recorded the words of Jesus which seemed to sum up his whole teaching:

> "The right time has come and the Kingdom of God is near! Turn away from your sins and believe the Good News!"
> (1.15)

Having put pen to paper, Mark did not attempt to write a balanced biography of Jesus. He focused on little more than a year out of his life, and nearly half (40%) of his Gospel describes the last few days when Jesus was in or near Jerusalem and approaching death. Our curiosity about the birth, childhood and home background of Jesus is not satisfied in any way. Mark tells us nothing, either, about the parents of Jesus – Mary and Joseph – as Jesus suddenly emerges from total obscurity to be baptised at the age of 30 by John the Baptist in the River Jordan (1.9–11).

The reason for these curious omissions is that Mark was writing as a member of the Christian community which had already existed for over 30 years. This community had accepted from the beginning that Jesus was the Son of God, the Son of Man and the Messiah. There was no need for Mark to prove these truths to the early Christians but only to explain to them what they meant. The Christians knew that the death of Jesus was not an accident, but part of the plan and purpose of God. This is why Mark alone included the highly significant words of Jesus:

> "the Son of Man [Jesus] did not come to be served; he came to serve and to give his life to redeem many people."
> (10.45)

Jesus was sent by God to die. It was as simple as that to Mark.

The sources of information

Mark probably lived in Jerusalem and was a travelling companion of Paul, before he fell out with the apostle. Christian tradition links Mark with Peter, the leading disciple of Jesus and the leader of the early Christians. According to this tradition, Mark was Peter's helper in the early days. During this time, it seems, Peter passed much of his own very valuable information about Jesus on to Mark. Often Peter told these stories when he was preaching to the crowds, and Mark probably noted them down. Mark's link with Peter gave his Gospel very considerable authority in the early Church.

The Synoptic Gospels

There are four Gospels in the New Testament – Matthew, Mark, Luke and John – and the first three of these bear a close resemblance to each other, sharing many verses and stories. Because of this similarity they are called the Synoptic ('seeing together') Gospels. Both Matthew and Luke, who wrote around 80 CE, used Mark, since all but 31 verses in Mark's Gospel have a parallel in the other two. Mark, then, provides us with the earliest written information that we have about Jesus (apart from the scraps of information in Paul's writings), and that is what makes his Gospel so important.

Key Points

1 Jesus was crucified around 29 CE but the first Gospel, Mark's, was not written until about 65 CE. Until then the Christian message was largely kept alive by word of mouth.
2 Mark wrote at a time when the Church was undergoing persecution for the first time.
3 Mark's Gospel is not a balanced biography of Jesus. He concentrated on the last few

Mark devoted about 40% of his Gospel to the events leading up to and resulting from the death of Jesus.

days in his life because he believed that this was the most important part of the life of Jesus.
4 Mark relied heavily on Peter, the early Christian leader, for his information.
5 The Synoptic Gospels are Matthew, Mark and Luke. There is a close relationship between these three accounts. Mark's account is the earliest.

Work to do

1 Write down two reasons for saying that Mark was not trying to write a straightforward biography (life story) of Jesus in his Gospel.
2 What is meant by the 'oral transmission' of the Christian message?
3 Do you think that it makes any difference to the reliability of Mark's Gospel to point out that he was writing as a deeply committed member of the Christian community?

In the Glossary

Apostle • Gospel • Jerusalem • John • John the Baptist • Kingdom of God • Luke • Mark • Mary • Matthew • Messiah • New Testament • Paul • Peter • Son of Man • Synoptic Gospels

1.3 Jesus, man and God

Key Question

What did Mark want to teach his readers about Jesus of Nazareth?

The picture of Jesus given to us in Mark's Gospel reflects that held by the early Christians. On the one hand, Jesus was the Son of God who displayed all the authority that one would expect from God himself. On the other hand, he was very human and went through all of the normal emotions and feelings experienced by other people.

Jesus, the Son of God

The opening words of Mark's Gospel set the tone for much of what is to follow:

"This is the Good News about Jesus Christ, the Son of God."
(1.1)

Jesus in Mark's Gospel showed divine qualities by demonstrating God's power and authority in everything he did, and it was this that set him apart from the other religious leaders of his time. Wherever he went, Jesus showed that he was bringing in God's kingdom by teaching the people about God in a new way (1.22), healing those who were ill (1.31, 41–42) and casting demons out of those possessed by evil spirits (1.25–27).

The divine importance of Jesus as the Son of God is underlined by Mark in several ways in his Gospel:

1 Jesus was not a mere human being – he was God's Son. Mark shared this belief with the whole Christian community. The title was the one by which the voice of God had addressed Jesus at his baptism (1.11) and, again, at his Transfiguration (9.7). Before Jesus died on the cross, the Roman centurion, a Gentile, had recognised him as God's Son (15.39) in a moment of inspiration. (There is more about this important title of Jesus in Unit 2.)

2 Jesus had come to earth to establish God's kingdom (rule) in the hearts of all men and women who believed in him. Jesus told more than one parable to show how this, a central theme of Mark's Gospel, would happen. Just as God's kingdom was like a plant that grows slowly, but surely, beneath the earth's surface, so God's rule on earth will grow without people realising it.

This does not happen, though, without a real struggle – against sin, sickness and the powers of darkness. The growth of God's kingdom and the struggle between Jesus and all that is evil in the world is a frequent theme in Mark's Gospel.

3 To carry out God's work on earth Jesus had to serve others before suffering and dying for them. The opposition that Jesus faced brought about his death – and the same fate awaits many of his followers (8.31; 9.31; 10.33). Mark used this lesson to encourage those Christians who were suffering even as he wrote, and to stir up any Christian who might be contemplating giving up the faith because the cost of following Jesus as a disciple had become too great.

4 What happened to Jesus was both prophesied by the prophets of old and was part of God's plan. Mark frequently used the words 'It is written' to show the true meaning of the Jewish Scriptures, as he saw them, and to stress that God was always in control of events. Nothing happened in the life of Jesus by accident, and this was very comforting to those who found their own lives to be in great danger because of their faith.

5 People need to have faith in Jesus to be one of his followers. On one occasion

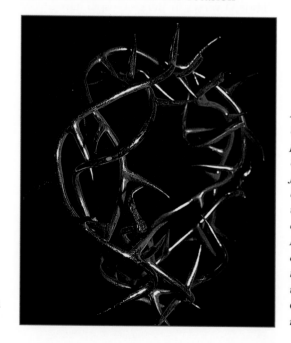

A crown of thorns was placed on the head of Jesus shortly before he was crucified. Mark emphasised that Jesus was both God and man.

mothers brought their little children so that Jesus could bless them, but they were turned away by his disciples who thought that Jesus was too busy to bother with them (10.13–16). Jesus was very angry when he saw this taking place; he told his disciples that no one could enter God's kingdom unless they showed the childlike trust (faith) of a little child. Most of the people who were healed by Jesus were required to show faith, although that faith was occasionally shown for them by someone else (2.1–12).

The human Jesus

Mark found the divine Jesus, the Son of God, very comforting. At the same time, however, he was not afraid to show us the other side of his personality. The same Jesus who showed his power over sickness and evil was also angry on occasions (9.19); spoke very sharply to Peter, one of his closest friends (8.33); grew impatient with his disciples (8.17–21); lost his temper with a barren fig-tree because he was hungry (11.14, 21); and was overcome with disappointment when God seemed to abandon him at his hour of greatest need (15.34). You can find out more about this in the information box below.

Mark believed the story of Jesus' suffering would encourage Christians to bear their own suffering too.

Key Points

1 Mark's picture of Jesus in his Gospel strongly reflects the beliefs of the early Christian Church.
2 Mark saw Jesus as the Son of God who showed divine power when he came to establish God's kingdom on earth. He came to fulfil the Jewish Scriptures.
3 Mark also saw Jesus as genuinely human. He displayed all the frailties of human nature.

For your Information

Here are four quotations from Mark's Gospel to show how he painted a very human picture of Jesus.

- 'Jesus was filled with pity, and stretched out his hand and touched him.' (1.41)

- 'But Jesus turned round, looked at his disciples, and rebuked Peter. "Get away from me, Satan," he said.' (8.33)

- 'Jesus said to the fig-tree, "No one shall ever eat figs from you again!"' (11.14)

- 'Jesus went to the Temple and began to drive out those who were buying and selling. He overturned the tables of the money-changers and the stools of those who sold pigeons.' (11.15)

In the Glossary

Baptism • Disciple • Gospel • Mark • Messiah • Parable • Peter • Prophet • Transfiguration

Work to do

1 a What does the word 'Messiah' mean?
   b By looking up Mark 8.27–30 discover which disciple of Jesus first recognised him as God's Messiah – and where.
   c What is God's kingdom and what kind of opposition does it meet on earth?
   d What fate, according to Mark's Gospel, might await those who follow Jesus, and why was this reminder so appropriate at the time?
2 Describe, in your own words, how Mark:
   a presents a very human picture of Jesus;
   b presents a clear picture of Jesus as the divine Son of God.
   Refer to at least two examples in Mark's Gospel in each case.
3 Explain how, in the opening verse to his Gospel, Mark introduces what is to follow.

1.4 The authority of Mark's Gospel

Key Question

How do Christians make use of Mark's Gospel today in their private devotions and in their public worship?

For most Christians all parts of the Bible are important because they tell the unfolding story of God's salvation – for the Jewish people and for Christian believers. Yet amongst the 66 books of the Bible (37 in the Old Testament and 29 in the New Testament) the Gospels are unique. This is why the Gospels are given a special place in all acts of Christian worship, both personal and communal.

Using the Gospels

At the heart of all Christian belief and worship stands the Trinity – God the Father, God the Son and God the Holy Spirit. Christians believe that God the Son, Jesus, came from the presence of God in heaven to reveal the Father's (God's) loving care for all of life on earth. In the Gospels, including Mark's, this love is shown in the teaching, miracles, love, suffering, death and resurrection of Jesus. Jesus is seen to be 'love in action'.

After Jesus left the earth at the end of his life, the Holy Spirit was given to humankind on the day of Pentecost to continue the work of love that Jesus had begun. Amongst other names, Jesus said that the Holy Spirit would be the 'Comforter' and the 'Helper'. He is often pictured in churches as a dove, the bringer of peace to the world. Christians believe that the Holy Spirit is still present and active in the world today, making God known to all who believe. He continues to be with all those who seek to serve God, by providing them with divine strength and guidance.

Because of the importance of Jesus to their faith, Christians want to learn all that they can about him. To do this they read and study the four Gospels in the New Testament. These Gospels, especially John's, present readers with their own, very individual, pictures of Jesus. At the same time, when they are brought together, they provide us with our only real portrait of Jesus. We know very little about Jesus from any other source. Mark's Gospel, as the shortest of the four Gospels, is one of the most widely used parts of the Bible. It plays an important part in both personal devotion and public acts of worship.

Personal devotion

Most Christians spend time regularly reading their Bible as they believe that this is the main way in which God speaks to them today. Through reading Mark's Gospel they are reminded of the teachings and actions of Jesus. They are also encouraged to reflect deeply on the meaning of his life, death and resurrection, and they are led to find out more about what it means to be a Christian disciple in the modern world.

Christians also study the life of Jesus with other like-minded believers. In many churches Lent, the 40 days of preparation which lead up to Easter, is used to bring people together to study a part of the Bible. As Lent leads up to a celebration and remembrance of the death and resurrection of Jesus, so this is an appropriate time to study those events from the Bible. Often Mark's account is chosen for this because it is briefer, and more direct, than the others. For the same reason a copy of Mark's Gospel is often given to new Christians to introduce them to the Bible.

Since the birth of the Christian Church a dove has been the most common symbol for the Holy Spirit.

Public acts of worship

Reading the Bible aloud plays a very important part in every act of Christian worship or service. In many churches worshippers bring their own Bible with them to church so that they can follow the readings. In Anglican and Roman Catholic churches a lectionary (set order) of readings is followed in church, which takes worshippers through much of the Bible over a period of time. In the Eucharist and the Mass, services which celebrate the death of Jesus in Jerusalem, there are three Bible readings – one from the Old Testament, one from the Epistles and one from the Gospels. The first two of these readings are usually delivered by someone from the congregation (a layperson), but the Gospel reading is always given by the priest. For this the Bible is often carried in a procession to the centre of the church above the heads of the worshippers, where it is held by a server as it is read. This underlines the importance of the Gospel reading.

In many churches a special service is held during the most solemn day in the Christian year – Good Friday. This is the day on which Christians throughout the world commemorate the death of Jesus on the cross. In this special service, called a 'vigil' (watching), members of the congregation 'watch' with Jesus between noon and 3.00 p.m. during the last hours of his life. Just as the Gospels tell us that a group of women stayed with Jesus during this time, so Christians do the same today. During this service the whole description of events leading up to Jesus' death, and the death itself, is read from the Gospels – often Mark's.

Key Points

1 The Gospels are used widely by Christians because they are the Church's 'source documents'. They outline the part played by God the Father, God the Son and God the Holy Spirit in the work of salvation.
2 Most Christians spend time studying the Bible – especially the Gospels. This is particularly true during the season of Lent. Often Mark's Gospel is chosen to be read at this time because it is briefer than the others.
3 Reading the Bible is also very important in Christian worship, especially in the services leading up to Easter. The Gospels form the heart of these readings.

Work to do

1 List two ways in which the importance of reading from the Gospels is underlined in church.
2 a From where do Christians obtain their only detailed knowledge of the life and teaching of Jesus?
　b Why do most Christians spend time regularly reading the Bible?
　c What is Lent?
　d Why do many churches use the season of Lent to encourage Christians to meet together to study the Bible?
3 Why do you think that many church services include Bible readings from the Old Testament, the Epistles and the Gospels in their services?

In the Glossary

Anglican Church • Bible • Easter • Epistle • Eucharist • Good Friday • Gospel • Holy Spirit • Holy Week • John • Lent • Mark • Mass • New Testament • Old Testament • Pentecost • Priest • Roman Catholic Church • Trinity

The public reading of the Bible, especially the Gospels, has always been a central part of Christian worship.

1.5 Interpreting Mark's Gospel

Key Question

What are the different approaches that Christians adopt to the four Gospels?

In Orthodox services the book of the Gospels is kissed to show the high respect in which it is held.

The four Gospels are particularly important to Christian believers. They are the only books which contain detailed records of what Jesus said and did. Mark's Gospel is particularly important because it is widely recognised to be the earliest of the four descriptions and so is the nearest in time to the events that it describes. It was also based on the recollections and observations of Peter who was the best placed of the disciples to know and understand the mind of Jesus.

For these reasons it is important for Christians to be able to rely on the information that Mark provides. This does not mean, though, that all Christians approach this Gospel, or the other Gospels, in the same way. At least three different ways of approaching the Gospels are adopted:

1 The Liberal approach. There are many Christians who believe that the Gospel writers were describing what they saw and understood – but that they might have been mistaken in some of the things they wrote. Liberals believe that Jesus used many different ways of teaching – such as through parables and startling sayings – which it

would be a mistake to understand literally. Indeed, to do so would be to miss a much more important, and deeper, meaning. An example of this might be the all-important Christian belief that Jesus rose from the dead after his crucifixion. Some Christians do not find it necessary to believe that the body of Jesus actually rose from the grave. It is enough for them to believe that the teaching and inspiration of Jesus lives on today and that is what really matters about the event.

2 The Conservative approach. The Conservatives believe that the Gospel writers were recording the 'truth' as God made this known to them. Clearly the Bible was pre-scientific and this may cause some problems, but Conservatives believe that its text is still very reliable and accurate. According to this view we can turn to the Gospels for a totally reliable record of the teachings and life of Jesus.

Some Christians take the words of the Bible literally.

3 The Fundamentalist and Literalist approaches. Fundamentalists believe that the Bible was dictated by God to men who wrote down what they were told. They were little more than secretaries. This means, of course, that the record of the Bible is absolutely accurate. This includes those parts of the Bible, such as the miracles of Jesus, which many modern people may find it very difficult to accept.

Literalists are fundamentalists who take their understanding of the Bible a stage further. In the ending (16.9–20) which is added to Mark's Gospel in some old manuscripts, and which is not thought to be by Mark, the followers of Jesus are promised that they will be able to pick up deadly snakes and drink poison without suffering any bad consequences. For a small number of Christians this promise can be taken at its face value.

The Bible as the Word of God

Most Christians believe that the Bible is the 'Word of God'. At the end of most public readings of the Bible in church services the words are added 'This is the Word of God'. They disagree, however, over just what these words mean. Clearly all Christians expect to learn something about God and Jesus from listening to the Bible. In that sense the Bible is accepted by all as being 'God's Word'. There is a message in the Bible which

remains true for Christians through every period of history – even though our knowledge and understanding of life and the world may be changing and growing all the time.

Key Points

1 Most Christians believe that the Bible is the Word of God but they do not all understand this in the same way.
2 Liberals accept that there may be mistakes in the Bible but that the meaning of a passage is what really matters – not its detail.
3 Conservatives stress the reliability of the Bible – it can be trusted in its detail.
4 Fundamentalists and Literalists are committed to the absolute reliability of the Biblical text since it was dictated by God in the first place.

Work to do

1 Give two reasons why the Gospel of Mark is particularly important to most Christians.
2 Write two sentences about each of the following:
   a The Liberal approach to the Bible.
   b The Conservative approach to the Bible.
   c The Fundamentalist and Literalist approach to the Bible.

Key Question

What did the early Christians mean when they spoke of Jesus as the Son of God?

The title 'Son of God', applied to Jesus, only occurs in Mark's Gospel eight times. You can find these occasions listed in the information box. Yet the 'Son of God' is used at crucial times by Mark, suggesting that this title, more than any other, summed up for him the ministry of Jesus. It is there in the opening line of the Gospel (1.1), whilst the confession of the Roman centurion, a Gentile, at the foot of the cross (15.39) comes at the climax of Jesus' death. It is a kind of epitaph on the whole life and ministry of Jesus. As God's Son, Jesus had a special role to play on earth and a special relationship with God – as Mark makes very clear in his Gospel.

Jesus as God's Son

The first clue that we have to understanding the title 'Son of God' is found in the Old Testament, where people who were close to God, and had a special relationship with him, were called 'sons of God'. At different times in the Jewish Scriptures the title was applied to the angels in heaven, the nation of Israel and even judges and rulers. When the title was given to Jesus, in the New Testament, it indicated that he was God's representative on earth with a special God-given mission to carry out. Yet Jesus was not just one of the many sons of God. To Mark, Jesus' relationship with God was unique and quite unlike that enjoyed by any other human being – or angel! Jesus was one with God. Jesus was God.

At the beginning of his Gospel, Mark presents Jesus as the one who has 'come' from God (1.9), and after his death he returned home to his Father God in heaven (14.62). In between, during his time on earth, this special relationship between God and Jesus broke through from time to time – a fact that was recognised by those men and women who responded to Jesus with amazement. They were amazed by the God-like qualities that Jesus displayed by his words and actions. Mark tells us that this happened:

- following many miracles (e.g. 1.27; 2.12);
- as a response to the extraordinary teaching of Jesus which was unlike that of any other rabbi or teacher (e.g. 1.22; 6.2);
- after Jesus had shown himself to be God's Son (e.g. 4.41; 6.50, 51);
- after Jesus had spoken to his disciples about his future suffering (e.g. 9.32; 10.32).

It is strange to notice that the disciples never once referred to Jesus as God's Son – although evil spirits did (1.24; 3.11) and Jesus used the title of himself more than once (12.6; 13.32). The title was also used by the High Priest when Jesus was being tried (14.61), and by God himself (1.11; 9.7).

The baptism and Transfiguration

Two episodes in Mark's Gospel – the baptism (see Unit 9.3) and Transfiguration (see Unit 2.2) – were particularly important in showing that Jesus was God's Son. His baptism by John the Baptist in the River Jordan (1.9–11) publicly announced that Jesus had come to bring God's kingdom. As Jesus came up out of the waters of the river, a voice from heaven announced to Jesus alone:

> "You are my own dear Son. I am pleased with you."
> (1.11)

For many people the resurrection of Jesus from the dead is the main reason for believing him to be God's Son.

The Transfiguration of Jesus (9.2–8), an event that stands at the heart of Mark's Gospel, shows what it means to call Jesus 'God's Son'. It introduces the two greatest Old Testament prophets, Moses and Elijah, to support that claim and, again, 'the voice of God' adds its own witness. Having seen Jesus revealed as God's Son on this occasion, though, Mark immediately reminds his readers that they must keep their minds on the suffering of Jesus which lay just around the corner. That suffering, and death, take up a large part of Mark's Gospel. We will look at the Transfiguration of Jesus in the next unit.

For your Information

In Mark's Gospel Jesus is called 'the Son of God' in the following places:

a 'This is the Good News about Jesus Christ, the Son of God!' (1.1)

b 'You are my own dear Son. I am pleased with you.' (1.11)

c 'And whenever the people who had evil spirits in them saw him, they would fall down before him and scream, "You are the Son of God!"' (3.11)

d '… he ran, fell on his knees before him, and screamed in a loud voice, "Jesus, Son of the Most High God!"' (5.6–7)

e '… a voice came from the cloud, "This is my own dear Son – listen to him!"' (9.7)

f 'No one knows, however, when that day or hour will come – neither the angels in heaven, nor the Son; only the Father knows.' (13.32)

g 'Are you the Messiah, the Son of the Blessed God?' (14.61)

h 'This man was really the Son of God!' (15.39)

Key Points

1 The phrase 'Son of God' is used sparingly in Mark's Gospel. It always indicates that Jesus is believed to be divine.
2 The disciples did not use this title of Jesus.
3 The baptism and Transfiguration of Jesus both emphasised his divine origin.

Work to do

1 Look up and describe two occasions on which Mark says that the people responded to Jesus with amazement.
2 Explain:
   a what is meant when the title 'Son of God' is applied to Jesus in Mark's Gospel;
   b how the term 'sons of God' was applied to people in the Old Testament and what was meant by it.

In the Glossary

Baptism • Disciple • Elijah • Gospel • High Priest • Icon • John the Baptist • Mark • Moses • Old Testament • Prophet • Rabbi • Transfiguration

Icons are spiritual paintings, used mainly in the Orthodox Church as aids to personal devotion. Many of the icons represent Jesus as the son of God.

2.2 The Transfiguration of Jesus

 Read

Mark
9.2–13

 **Key Question**

What did Mark want his readers to learn from the story of the Transfiguration of Jesus?

Peter, James and John formed an 'inner circle' amongst the disciples of Jesus, spending much time alone with him. They shared with him some of the most important events in his life (see the information box). For the Transfiguration of Jesus, one of the most mysterious events in the Gospels, the four of them climbed together up the lower slopes of Mount Hermon, a snow-capped mountain 2,800 feet high on Israel's northern border. While they were alone with Jesus the three disciples saw a vision and heard a voice from heaven – clues which were intended to remind readers of the earlier baptism of Jesus.

The cloud

Mark's Jewish readers were very familiar with their own Scriptures and knew that their ancestor, Moses, had been summoned by God to meet with him on a mountain. This happened as the Jews were travelling from slavery in Egypt to the Promised Land of Canaan – a journey known as the 'Exodus'. As Moses climbed the mountain to meet God, cloud covered it for six days; on the seventh, God spoke to him out of the cloud. In the Old Testament few people were privileged to speak to God, and no one was allowed to see him directly since his glory was thought to be too great for human eyes to bear.

Whenever anyone, such as Moses, approached to speak with him, God was always covered by a cloud to hide his glory. Even then, six days of purification (cleansing) were needed before any conversation could take place. Mark linked this event involving Moses with the one he is about to describe, by telling us that Jesus too heard God speak to him from a cloud after six days of waiting.

The Transfiguration

Whilst on the mountain with Jesus, the three disciples saw that his appearance changed (was 'transfigured') in front of them. The 'dazzling white' of his clothing is typical in the Bible of angels and other heavenly beings. For a brief moment they saw Jesus as he really was – the Son of God – talking with two of the most important Jewish leaders from the past, Moses and Elijah.

Moses was the great law-giver and prophet responsible for passing on the Torah (the Law) to the Jewish people. The Torah was the greatest gift that God had given to the Jewish nation.

Elijah was the most important prophet in Jewish history. He was the prophet who, in Jewish belief, would return to earth to announce the arrival of God's long-awaited Messiah. On more than one occasion in the Gospels Elijah was likened to John the Baptist.

The disciples were so frightened by their experience that they did not know what to say. Peter broke the silence by offering to build shelters (tabernacles) for Jesus, Moses and Elijah on the mountain. Jews built and decorated special huts or shelters in their homes using leaves and branches during the annual festival of Tabernacles. They ate and prayed in the huts to remind themselves of the shelters that their ancestors had built in the desert after they left Egyptian slavery. Jews today still recall this journey every time they celebrate the festival. It is very likely that the Transfiguration took place during the festival of Tabernacles.

A voice from heaven

A voice from the cloud spoke to all of them:

"This is my own dear son – listen to him!" (9.7)

The words are almost identical to those that Jesus heard at his baptism (see Unit 9.3). Here the words left the disciples in no doubt that Jesus was God's son. The voice told them to listen very carefully to what Jesus had to say and, as 8.31 makes clear, this refers to the words that Jesus spoke about his future death in Jerusalem. On the way down from the mountain Jesus ordered his disciples to say nothing about this experience 'until the Son of Man [Jesus] has risen from death' (9.9).

For your Information

The inner circle of disciples – Peter, James and John – alone are present with Jesus on three occasions in Mark's Gospel:

a when Jesus restored the dead girl to life (5.21–43);

b at the Transfiguration (9.2–13);

c in the Garden of Gethsemane (14.32–42).

Key Points

1 The three disciples involved in the Transfiguration of Jesus formed a kind of 'inner circle' among the disciples.
2 The cloud in the Transfiguration was symbolically important – it hid the overwhelming majesty of God.
3 Moses and Elijah represented the Law and the Prophets from the Old Testament.
4 The voice from heaven was a reminder of what happened at the baptism of Jesus.

Work to do

1 a Where did the Transfiguration of Jesus take place?
  b What does the word 'Transfiguration' mean?
  c Who was with Jesus when the Transfiguration took place?
  d What did Peter ask?
  e What words were spoken to Jesus out of the cloud?
  f What was the importance of the Transfiguration to Mark and the early Christians?
2 Describe, in detail, the Transfiguration of Jesus.
3 Explain two possible ways of approaching the story of the Transfiguration of Jesus.

In the Glossary

Baptism • Disciple • Elijah • Exodus • Gospel • James • Jerusalem • John • Mark • Moses • Old Testament • Peter • Prophet • Torah • Transfiguration

For many Christians it does not matter whether the Transfiguration of Jesus was an actual event or a vision that took place in the minds of the disciples.

2.3 The Son of Man

Read

Isaiah
53.1–9

Daniel 7.14

Mark 8.31;
10.45

Key Question

Why did Jesus often call himself the 'Son of Man', and what did he understand by this title?

On 13 separate occasions in Mark's Gospel Jesus referred to himself as the Son of Man (see information box). It was his favourite way of describing himself but, surprisingly, no one else called him by this title.

The Son of Man in the Old Testament

Mark wrote his Gospel mainly for the church in Rome, which was made up of both Jewish and Gentile Christians. A Gospel for such a mixed church would need to explain Jewish ideas carefully so that non-Jewish readers could understand them. At the same time, Mark did not show the same interest in the Jewish Scriptures as Matthew did in his Gospel, since they would not have interested Gentile Christians so much.

Yet, at times, it is necessary to go back into the Old Testament to understand some of the central ideas in the teaching of Jesus. This is certainly the case with the title 'Son of Man'. In the Old Testament, where the phrase was widely used, it had two distinct meanings:

1 The phrase 'son of man' was used generally to describe any member of the human race. The Psalmist used it in this way when he asked God:

> "What is man [the son of man], that you think of him; mere man, that you care for him?"
> (Psalm 8.4)

In Ezekiel the phrase crops up no fewer than 93 times, and each time the reference is to the prophet himself. God frequently addresses Ezekiel as 'mortal man' or 'son of man', emphasising the humanness of the prophet, mortal and sinful, totally dependent on God.

2 A very different idea of the 'Son of Man' comes from Daniel, which was probably the last book in the Old Testament to be written, in the 2nd century BCE. Daniel described a vision in which a glorious being 'like the Son of Man' descends from heaven to rule on earth (Daniel 7.14, 15). This figure is superhuman, divine and eternal – existing

from the time before God created the world. The Son of Man entered God's presence and was given authority over God's kingdom. The Son of Man then remains hidden until the end of time, when he appears with his angels to judge the human race. There are some real clues in Daniel as to how Jesus saw his work on earth – and beyond. Yet, there is no indication in Daniel that the Son of Man was to be a suffering figure, as Jesus was to be.

The Son of Man in Mark's Gospel

The many sayings about the Son of Man in Mark's Gospel reflect the importance that the early Church placed upon this title of Jesus. The sayings fall into three groups which convey important aspects of Jesus' work and significance:

1 The Son of Man (Jesus) had the power (authority) on earth to forgive sins. Often in Mark's Gospel a person's body is healed after their sins have been forgiven. In Mark's account of the healing of the paralysed man (2.1–12), for instance, Jesus told the man that his sins had been forgiven before his

Mark linked the idea of Jesus suffering on the cross and dying with the title 'Son of Man'.

body was healed. This brought the charge, from some teachers of the Law, that he was blaspheming since only God had the power to forgive sins. In reply Jesus asked them:

> "Is it easier to say to this paralysed man, 'Your sins are forgiven', or to say, 'Get up, pick up your mat, and walk?' I will prove to you, then, that the Son of Man has authority on earth to forgive sins."
> (2.9–10)

2 The Son of Man must suffer, die and rise again from the dead. This new and striking idea was based on Isaiah's picture of God's Servant (the Messiah) who would suffer and die rather than lead the Jews in triumph against their enemies. This comes out clearly on the three occasions when Jesus spoke to his disciples about his forthcoming death (8.31–38; 9.30–32; 10.32–34). No talk there of victory or triumph – only of suffering and death.

3 The Son of Man will appear at the end of time 'seated on the right of the Almighty and coming with the clouds of heaven' (14.62). Whilst this idea was prominent in Jewish writings, Christians believed that the Son of Man was actually Jesus – which Jews did not. Christians call the future time when Jesus will return to earth 'the Second Coming'. Many of them still look forward to this event.

Christians believe that the Son of Man, Jesus, will return to earth and that everyone will appear before him to be judged.

For your Information

The references to the Son of Man in Mark's Gospel fall into three categories:

a The authority of Jesus on earth to forgive sins – the paralysed man healed (2.10); the question of the Sabbath day (2.28).

b The suffering, death and resurrection of Jesus – warning his disciples about future suffering (8.31; 8.38; 9.9, 12, 31; 10.33, 45; 14.21, 41).

c The future return to Jesus to the earth – returning in great glory (13.26; 14.62).

Key Points

1 'Son of Man' was the favourite title of Jesus for himself, but no one else used it for him.
2 The title had deep roots in the Old Testament where it meant both an ordinary man and a superhuman figure.
3 In Mark the Son of Man was a God figure who had the authority to forgive sins.
4 The Son of Man was also tragic figure who would die and rise again.

Work to do

1 a Sum up, in two sentences, what you think the phrase 'Son of Man' means.
  b Why do you think that Jesus was very fond of calling himself the Son of Man?
  c What can we learn about the meaning of the phrase 'Son of Man' from Daniel 7.13–14?
2 Describe the two ways in which the phrase 'Son of Man' was used in the Old Testament.
3 The phrase 'Son of Man' conveyed three important aspects of the work of Jesus. What were they?
4 Describe two occasions in Mark where Jesus calls himself the 'Son of Man'.

In the Glossary

Angel • Blasphemy • Gospel • Mark • Old Testament • Prophet • Second Coming • Son of Man

2.4 Healing the paralysed man

Read

Mark
2.1–12

Key Question

What is the key point that Mark makes in his description of Jesus healing a paralysed man?

After trying to establish the authority of Jesus as a healer at the beginning of his Gospel, Mark moved on to describe the growing antagonism of the religious authorities towards him. Between 2.1 and 3.6 he included five 'conflict-stories', which are grouped together by their common theme of conflict between Jesus and the religious authorities (see information box). These stories were probably used by Christian teachers at the time to warn young converts that they could expect opposition – just like Jesus. By the end of these stories the Pharisees and the Herodians were plotting together to kill Jesus (3.6).

The paralysed man

The first conflict-story, that of Jesus healing the paralysed man (2.1–12), is unique since it is the only place in Mark's Gospel where Jesus claims to have the authority to forgive sins. When the people in Capernaum heard that Jesus was in the town, 'the news spread that he was at home'(2.1). In fact, he was probably in the home of Simon Peter and Andrew (see 1.29). Whilst there, Jesus preached about the Kingdom of God but was interrupted by four men bringing a paralysed friend on a stretcher to him. Unable to find a way through the large crowd, the men let their friend down to the feet of Jesus through the roof. This was not as difficult as it sounds since the flat roofs of Palestinian houses were only covered with a thin layer of beaten earth mixed with straw and could be easily rolled back.

It was the faith of the four friends that so impressed Jesus. All of the miracles in Mark's Gospel demand real faith: such dependence formed a bridge between Jesus and the person who sought healing. Here, uniquely, that faith is provided by other people and not by the person in need. Jesus rewarded their faith by saying to the paralytic:

> "My son, your sins are forgiven."
> (2.5)

The authority of Jesus

The miracle, however, only serves to introduce a conflict with the religious authorities, which revolved around the authority of Jesus to forgive sins. The basic argument of the scribes, who have already been compared unfavourably with Jesus (1.22), was that no one could forgive sins except God. For assuming this authority, Jesus is accused by the scribes of blasphemy – claiming to be God. Jesus put a question to them:

> "Is it easier to say to this paralysed man, 'Your sins are forgiven,' or to say, 'Get up, pick up your mat, and walk'?"
> (2.8)

Jesus then carried out the more difficult task (healing the paralytic) to show that he could meet the easier challenge (forgiving sins). As Jesus said:

> "I will prove to you, then, that the Son of Man has authority on earth to forgive sins."
> (2.10)

This priest has the Church's authority to hear the confession of sins and to forgive them in God's name.

Mark's readers, and the Christian community, believed that the power to heal did not disappear when Jesus left the earth. The Church has always believed that it has the power both to forgive sins and to heal those in need (see photographs). This work continues today in many churches.

For your Information

Mark grouped together five stories at the start of his Gospel which showed Jesus coming into conflict with the religious authorities. He wanted to show that Jesus encountered real opposition almost from the moment that he stepped on to the public stage. These 'conflict-stories' are:

a The healing of the paralysed man – conflict with 'teachers of the Law' (scribes) (2.1–12).

b Eating a meal in Levi's house after he had called him to be a disciple – conflict with 'teachers of the Law, who were Pharisees' (2.13–17).

c A dispute about fasting – conflict with those who wondered why his disciples did not fast whilst the disciples of John the Baptist and the Pharisees did (2.18–20).

d A dispute about the Sabbath day after his disciples ate some corn on the holy day – conflict with Pharisees (2.23–28).

e Healing the man with the paralysed hand on the Sabbath day – conflict with Pharisees (3.1–6).

Key Points

1 There are several 'conflict-stories' in Mark's Gospel which show Jesus coming into conflict with the religious authorities. This is one such story.
2 In the miracle of the paralysed man Jesus claimed to have the power to forgive sins – a power given to God alone.
3 The paralysed man was brought to Jesus by four friends – it was their faith that so impressed Jesus.
4 Because he claimed to be able to forgive sins Jesus was accused of blasphemy by his enemies.
5 The healing ministry of Jesus is still continued by the Christian Church today.

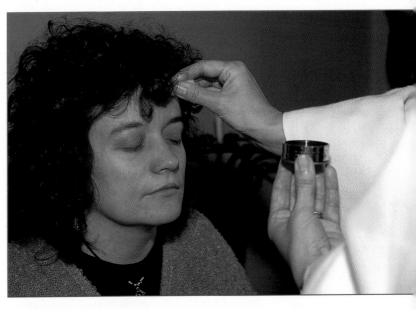

Anointing a sick person with oil and praying for healing are two activities still carried on by many churches today.

Work to do

1 a What do you think 'faith' is?
 b How important was faith in the cure of the paralysed man?
 c Whose faith was it that brought about the healing of this man, and how did it show itself?
2 a Why do you think it would have been easier to have said that the man's sins were forgiven than to have healed him?
 b How did Jesus explain the link between healing the paralysed man and forgiving his sins?
3 Many people in the time of Jesus thought that illness was the direct result of sinful behaviour.
 a Why do you think they thought this?
 b Do you think there is any truth in this idea?
 c Is there any reason for thinking that this belief might be behind the story of the healing of the paralysed man?

In the Glossary

Andrew • Blasphemy • Gospel • Herodians • John the Baptist • Kingdom of God • Mark • Peter • Pharisees • Sabbath day • Scribe • Son of Man

2.5 True greatness

Read

Mark
9.33–37;
10.35–45

Key Question

What impossible request did James and John make of Jesus – and how did he respond to it?

Jesus used the example of a small child to teach his disciples about humility and true greatness.

There are two stories in Mark's Gospel involving the disciples of Jesus which revolve around the twin issues of greatness and places of honour in God's kingdom. This was a matter of some importance to the disciples. They wanted to be sure that they were going to be rewarded for leaving everything to follow Jesus. Clearly such a reward was not going to come in this life, but would they be given special treatment in the life to come? This concern of the disciples stands in stark contrast to Jesus himself who, as the Son of Man, has come to serve others, to suffer and die. This was something that it took the disciples a long time to learn.

Who is the greatest?

Jesus and his disciples were on their way to Jerusalem. Jesus had just predicted, for a second time, that he was to be arrested, tried, condemned and killed by his enemies (9.30–32). Mark tells us that the disciples did not understand what Jesus was talking about on this occasion, as on the first, and they were afraid to ask him. Instead they preferred to argue amongst themselves as to which one of them was the greatest. To answer their question Jesus taught them the link between spiritual greatness and humility. He told them:

"Whoever wants to be first must place himself last of all and be the servant of all."
(9.35)

He then used a small child to teach his disciples a lesson in humility and real greatness. A child is the weakest member of a community and needs constant protection. Looking after and caring for these children was a God-given task. To love the weak and provide that protection, he told them, was to serve and love God himself. In fact, God came to them in the form of a little child. Love the child, and they would be loving God himself. This is why Jesus told his disciples:

"Whoever welcomes in my name one of these children, welcomes me; and whoever welcomes me, welcomes not only me but also the one who sent me."
(9.37)

The request of James and John

James and John, who with Peter formed the 'inner circle' of disciples, approached Jesus with an impossible request. They wanted to be given the best seats when Jesus entered into his glory in heaven (10.37). Jesus told them that they did not understand what they were asking. He spoke to them of the cup that he must drink and the baptism through which he must pass – symbols for the passion and suffering that lay ahead of him in Jerusalem.

The cup was a familiar Jewish symbol. It was used in the Old Testament to indicate both joy (Psalm 116.13) and disaster (Jeremiah 25.15). It was also a symbol of the suffering to come in the Garden of Gethsemane, where Jesus asked God that the cup of suffering be taken from him (14.36).

James and John did not understand what Jesus was talking about. This theme of Jesus being misunderstood by his disciples is one that Mark returns to time and time again. Here, while promising James and John that they will share his suffering (James was martyred in 54 CE), Jesus tells them that the

Jesus used a wine goblet to speak of the suffering ('the cup of suffering') that he must soon go through.

positions of highest honour in heaven are not his to give. God alone is responsible for distributing them, and there is nothing Jesus can do to influence that.

The disciples

The discussion widened out at this point to include the other disciples, who were very annoyed with James and John. To answer them Jesus gives them a lesson in humble service – and deals with the meaning of his own death at the same time. He tells them that there is a great difference between the Kingdom of God and any human kingdom. In God's kingdom it is service, not power, that matters. Even God's Son, the Son of Man, has come to serve others and give his life so that they might live (10.45). Those who are his real disciples might be called upon to suffer as well. They are certainly called by God to serve those around them – whether they are friends or enemies.

The disciples were slowly being forced to change their ideas about the Messiah and the work he had come to do. However, there was still a long way to go before they could accept the truth that the Son of Man had come to earth specifically to die for others.

Key Points

1 Jesus used himself as the perfect example of service to others. He also used a small child to show what true humility and greatness meant.
2 James and John requested that they be given the best seats in heaven. Jesus told them that they had been chosen to suffer for their faith. That is the only path to true greatness. James and John did not understand what Jesus was saying.
3 In God's kingdom the Son of Man had come to serve others. That was true greatness. The dying Son of Man was a message that the disciples took a very long time to learn.

Work to do

1 Only Mark records these words:

"if one of you wants to be first, he must be the slave of all."
(10.44)

a Who said these words?
b To whom was he speaking?
c What lessons were drawn from the incident?

2 We do not know whether these words actually came from Jesus or from Mark, but they do sum up his life:

"For even the Son of Man did not come to be served; he came to serve and to give his life to redeem many people."
(10.45)

a Why do you think that Jesus is called the Son of Man in this extract?
b Why do you think that the statement includes the word 'even'?
c How do these words seem to sum up the life, and death, of Jesus?

3 a Describe the request that James and John asked of Jesus.
b Why did Jesus tell the two disciples that he could not grant them their request?
c How did Jesus use the request of James and John to teach the disciples a very important lesson?

In the Glossary

Disciple • Jerusalem • John • Kingdom of God • Mark • Messiah • Old Testament • Peter • Son of Man

2.6 Jesus predicts his own death

Read

Mark
8.31–33;
9.30–32;
10.32–34

**Key
Question**

How did
Jesus try to
warn his
disciples of
what lay
ahead, and
why did
they fail to
understand
him?

Mark made it clear from the beginning of his Gospel that Jesus knew what lay ahead of him at the end of his life – arrest, trial and death. On three specific ocasions Jesus tried to warn his disciples of what was going to happen to the Son of Man – and each time they failed to understand what he was saying to them.

The first warning (8.31–33)

The first warning of Jesus follows a turning-point in Mark's Gospel, when Peter identified Jesus as God's Messiah at Caesarea Philippi (see Unit 2.11). Immediately after Peter's words, Jesus told his disciples that the Son of Man will:

> "suffer much and be rejected by the elders, the chief priests, and the teachers of the Law. He will be put to death, but three days later he will rise to life."
> (8.31)

To leave his readers in little doubt that he was recording the actual words of Jesus, Mark added:

> "He made this very clear to them."
> (8.32)

These words of Jesus were too much for Peter to take. He took Jesus to one side and began to 'rebuke' him. He tried to talk Jesus out of the path that would end with his rejection and death. In reply Jesus used the strongest possible language, calling Peter 'Satan' (the Devil) for suggesting evil thoughts to him. The disciple was seeing things from a human perspective and not God's point of view. Jesus had rejected the easy path when he resisted the temptations of Satan in the wilderness (see Unit 9.3) and would conquer any remaining doubts in the Garden of Gethsemane (12.1). He would not yield to the temptations of Satan – and neither must any would-be disciple. If it was God's will for Jesus to suffer and die then Peter would be very foolish to resist it.

Simon of Cyrene was helping Jesus to carry his cross. Peter was one of those who found it impossible to accept that Jesus was going to suffer a cruel death.

The second warning (9.30–32)

Later Jesus repeated his warning (that he would be put to death) and his promise (that three days later he would return to life) to his disciples:

> "The Son of Man will be handed over to men who will kill him. Three days later, however, he will rise to life."
> (9.31)

The time was fast approaching when events would be taken out of the hands of Jesus, and that was something the disciples found impossible to accept. The Romans controlled their conquered people through oppression and fear, but Jesus was offering them another way. Christian believers must serve others and give importance to those – like children and outsiders – who have no status in society (see 9.36). The Kingdom of God is for those who are powerless, and it is for these people that the Son of Man has come to suffer and die.

Children were an important part of the explanation that Jesus offered about why he had come to suffer and die.

The third warning (10.32–34)

Towards the end of his life Jesus knew that he must reach the city of Jerusalem quickly. Taking his disciples to one side, Jesus explained to them that the Son of Man would be handed over to the chief priests and teachers of the Law in Jerusalem, where he would be condemned to death. He would then be handed over to the Gentiles (Romans) who would mock him, spit on him and flog him. The Son of Man would be killed by his enemies, but would return to life three days later.

The warnings of Jesus seem very direct to us, but we have no way of knowing whether Mark is always reporting his exact words. He was writing more than 30 years after the event – and his reporting was certainly coloured elsewhere by what had happened to Jesus in the meantime. Even so, the failure of the disciples to understand Jesus is puzzling. Jesus had made many enemies during his short ministry and it was common knowledge that these very people were plotting his downfall. It seems as if the disciples deliberately shut their eyes to the truth – they could not bring themselves to believe that the Son of Man would suffer and die. They preferred to ignore the truth which was becoming clearer day by day.

Key Points

1 Jesus warned his disciples about his coming death for the first time just after Peter had made his declaration about Jesus at Caesarea Philippi.
2 On a second occasion Jesus again warned his disciples that he would be put to death but promised them that he would rise from the dead.
3 A little while later he warned his disciples again, saying that he must hurry to Jerusalem where he would be handed over to the chief priests and scribes.
4 Despite such clear warnings the disciples failed to grasp the truth of what Jesus was saying.

Work to do

1 Jesus warned his disciples that:

"we are going up to Jerusalem where the Son of Man will be handed over to the chief priests and the teachers of the Law. They will condemn him to death and then hand him over to the Gentiles, who will mock him, spit on him, whip him, and kill him; but three days later he will rise to life."
(10.33–34)

   a Why was Jerusalem an important city?
   b Who was the Son of Man?
   c What does the phrase 'handed over' suggest to you?
   d Who were the Gentiles in this case?
   e Which statement here suggests that it is God who is in control of events?
   f Why do some Christians suspect that Mark did not record the exact words of Jesus here?
2 Jesus spoke about his death to his disciples on more than one occasion.
   a Describe one occasion when he did this.
   b Explain why the disciples of Jesus seemed to have found his words about his forthcoming death hard to take in.

In the Glossary

Disciple • Gentile • Gospel • Jerusalem • Kingdom of God • Mark • Messiah • Peter • Satan • Son of Man

25

2.7 Calming the storm

 Read

**Mark
1.21–28;
4.35–41**

 **Key
Question**

**What value
did the
story of
Jesus
calming the
storm have
for the early
Christians?**

At the start of his ministry (1.21–28) Jesus had shown himself to be Lord over sickness and demons – two things that were closely connected with each other in the minds of people at the time. Now Jesus shows the same authority and control over the forces of nature, in a story that is vivid in eyewitness detail.

The creator of nature

Mark, like all Jews, believed that God was the creator and controller of nature. The Old Testament is full of stories which illustrate how he could use nature as he wished. God, for example, brought a succession of plagues on the Egyptians to persuade them to let the Israelites, their slaves, go (Exodus 7–11). A little later, God parted the waters of the Red Sea when the Egyptians were chasing the Israelites. The Israelites passed through safely but the Egyptians were drowned in the swirling waters.

Mark would expect Jesus, as God's representative on earth, to have similar power and authority. The nature miracles, those that show the authority of Jesus over nature, illustrate this. There are five nature miracles recorded in Mark's Gospel (see information box).

Calming the storm

The Jews were a people of the land who were terrified of water, especially the sea, since it was believed to be full of frightening creatures. Little wonder, then, that the disciples were terrified by this storm, although it probably did not threaten their lives. Mark, in his account, deals with the miracle as a kind of exorcism – a casting out of evil demons from the water. Jesus rebuked the winds and waves in the same way as he had earlier ordered demons to leave a man who was spirit-possessed (compare 1.25 with 4.39).

Although it was only an inland lake, the Sea of Galilee was renowned for its sudden, and fierce, squalls. As the wind howled and raged, Jesus slept on a cushion in the boat. This infuriated the disciples, who woke Jesus

up in a panic and questioned whether he cared for them. If he did, he would surely do something to save himself and them. To Mark, though, the sleeping of Jesus during the storm showed his complete faith in God, in stark contrast to the faithlessness of the disciples. It is a theme to which Mark was to return many times in his Gospel.

In the earlier story of the exorcism (1.21–28) Jesus responded to the evil spirit by commanding it to be quiet. In all exorcisms in the Gospels the lesser power (the evil spirit) has no alternative but to obey the greater power (Jesus) when he speaks with the authority of God. In this nature miracle Jesus commanded the wind to be silent and the waves to be still. He then rebuked and corrected his disciples with the same note of authority. He asked them:

> "Why are you frightened? Have you still no faith?"
> (4.40)

Mark relates the story of Jesus calming the storm as if it was an exorcism, a casting out of evil spirits.

This caused the disciples to be 'terribly afraid'. They had started off fearing the awesome power of nature, but they ended up fearing the authority of Jesus. As the disciples said:

> "Who is this man? Even the wind and the waves obey him!"
> (4.41)

The question went unanswered, but the answer is obvious. It is found in some words from the Old Testament:

> "The ships were lifted high in the air
>   and plunged down into the depths.
> In such danger the men lost their courage;
>   they stumbled and staggered like
>   drunken men …
> Then in their trouble they called to the Lord,
>   and he saved them from their distress.
> He calmed the raging storm,
>   and the waves became quiet."
> (Psalm 107.26–29)

For your Information

There are five nature miracles performed by Jesus in Mark's Gospel. They are:

- calming the storm (4.37–41)
- walking on water (6.45–51)
- feeding 5,000 people (6.31–44)
- feeding 4,000 people (8.1–9)
- the fig-tree withering (11.12–14, 20–25)

Key Points

1 The miracles of Jesus show that he had the same authority over the powers of nature as he did over sickness and death.
2 There are five nature miracles recorded by Mark.
3 In one miracle Jesus demonstrated his authority over a raging sea – an account which Mark relates as Jesus casting an evil spirit out of the sea. As in all miracles the greater power (Jesus) triumphs over the lesser power (the sea).

Work to do

1 a What is a nature miracle?
  b Which nature miracles are recorded by Mark in his Gospel?
  c Describe the occasion on which Jesus calmed a storm.
  d What was the reaction of the disciples to this miracle?
  e What did Mark intend his readers to learn from this miracle?
2 This quotation comes from the Old Testament:

> "Wake up, Lord! Why are you asleep? Rouse yourself! Don't reject us for ever!"
> (Psalm 44.23)

  Explain the link between this verse and Mark's account of the calming of the storm.
3 a What beliefs did Jews hold about the sea, and how are these beliefs reflected in the story of Jesus calming the storm?
  b Why do you think this story might have had special meaning for the early Christians undergoing a time of persecution?

In the Glossary

Disciple • Exorcism • Gospel • Mark • Old Testament

Storms at sea can be frightening, even for experienced fishermen.

2.8 Feeding a large crowd

 Read

Mark 6.31–44; 8.1–10

 **Key Question**

What was the significance of the occasions when Jesus fed a large crowd?

We have just discovered, in a long account (6.14–29), that John the Baptist has been put to death by Herod Antipas. John's death might have led some people to think that God was not in control of events at all. To counteract this suggestion, Mark includes two accounts which demonstrate God's power through Jesus over the world of nature.

Mark describes two occasions on which Jesus fed large groups of people miraculously, although the two descriptions almost certainly refer to the same event. In the first (6.31–44) Jesus fed 5,000 people, whilst in the second (8.1–10) 4,000 were miraculously provided with food to eat. As with two other nature miracles (4.35–41 and 6.45–52) the interest of Mark is mainly in the link between the events and the life of the Church. The two feeding accounts reminded readers of the Last Supper that Jesus shared with his disciples (14.12–26) and their own regular celebration of the Breaking of Bread – the Eucharist. This service is still at the heart of most Christian worship today (see Unit 8).

Feeding the 5,000

Mark does not say exactly where this miracle took place, although it was clearly in a remote place and close to the Sea of Galilee since Jesus set off by boat across the sea as soon as the people had been fed. The story begins with Jesus feeling sorry for the large crowd that had followed him for many hours – no doubt hoping to see a miracle. In a country where sheep and shepherds were very familiar sights, Mark described why Jesus felt so sorry for them in a graphic way:

> "When Jesus got out of the boat, he saw this large crowd, and his heart was filled with pity for them, because they were like sheep without a shepherd."
> (6.34)

He taught them, but when he had finished they were hungry and a long way from home. His disciples searched amongst the people and found no more than five loaves and two fish in the whole crowd.

They had come totally unprepared. In the sequence of events that followed:

1 Jesus took the five loaves and two fish in his hands, looked up to heaven, gave thanks and broke them. This is an accurate description of what happened at the start of a Breaking of Bread service, when the leader sought God's blessing on the elements of bread and wine.

2 The loaves and fish were then shared with all the people and 'everyone ate and had enough'(6.42). The disciples gathered together the fragments that were left over, and this amounted to 'twelve baskets full of what was left of the bread and the fish' (6.43). The mention of this detail underlines the miraculous nature of what had taken place.

There is an important link between Jesus feeding a large hungry crowd and the celebration of this Breaking of Bread service.

The amazing thing is that Mark made no mention of the reaction of the crowd to the miracle. Could they have been unaware, one wonders, of the miraculous events that were going on?

Understanding the miracle

The story of the feeding of the 5,000 was highly prized by the early Christians. It is uniquely recorded in all four of the Gospels and, if one includes the feeding of the 4,000, it is mentioned six times altogether (see information box). No other incident, apart from events in the last week of the life of Jesus, receives such extensive treatment in the Gospels. There are three main reasons why this story was so highly valued:

1 There is a strong parallel between Jesus miraculously feeding the crowd in a remote spot and God giving the Israelites manna in the wilderness during their journey from Egypt to the Promised Land. In one instance it is God feeding the needy and in the other, Jesus.

2 The story looked ahead to the time when Jesus shared the Last Supper with his disciples. In one bread and fish were shared, and in the other bread and wine, but both were blessed by Jesus in the same way. This meal is re-enacted every time that Christians come together to celebrate Holy Communion.

3 The story looked even further forward to the end of time. In Jewish and Christian tradition the Messiah would return to earth and give a banquet for those, alive and dead, who had been faithful to him. This miraculous feeding was a foretaste of that banquet.

For your Information

Descriptions of Jesus miraculously feeding large groups of people are found in the following places:

● The feeding of the 5,000: Matthew 14.15–21; Mark 6.31–44; Luke 9.12–17; John 6.5–13

● The feeding of the 4,000: Matthew 15.32–38; Mark 8.1–9

In the Glossary

Breaking of Bread • Disciple • Eucharist • Herod Antipas • Holy Communion • Last Supper • Mark • Messiah

Key Points

1 The miraculous feeding of a large crowd is a reminder of the Last Supper and the celebration of the service of Holy Communion.
2 This is the most widely reported miracle in the four Gospels.
3 The miracle looked forward to the time when the Messiah would return to earth and preside over a great banquet.

Work to do

1 In the story of the feeding of the 5,000:
  a Where did the incident take place?
  b Why was Jesus afraid to send the people home without feeding them first?
  c Why does Mark tells us that Jesus had compassion on the crowd, and which picture does he provide to illustrate this?
2 a What, in this event, reminds you of the Last Supper (look up 14.22–25)?
  b How did the Old Testament affect the way that Mark described Jesus feeding a large crowd?

Before feeding a large crowd Jesus suggested to his disciples that they should find food for the crowd to eat. This showed them the enormity of the miracle he was about to carry out.

2.9 Jesus and the Syro-Phoenician woman

Read

Mark
7.24–30

**Key
Question**

Why was the
healing of
the
daughter of
the Syro-
Phoenician
woman an
important
miracle and
what did it
show?

The healing of the daughter of the Syro-Phoenician woman is an important miracle in Mark's Gospel showing, as it did, more than one important theme in the ministry of Jesus. Before meeting the woman Jesus entered the region of Tyre where the population was, at least in part, non-Jewish. It was there that he met the woman who was described by Mark as being a Gentile (a non-Jew) from the Greek province of Syro-Phoenicia. The people would not have expected a woman with her background to have come into contact with a Jewish teacher.

The woman begged Jesus to heal her daughter. By this time it seems that his reputation as a healer had gone ahead of him and crossed national borders. Jesus may have been having a meal when the woman arrived and this would account for the conversation that followed.

Healing the woman's daughter

The woman begged Jesus to cast a demon out of her daughter. All manner of symptoms on those days were put down to demon-possession and we are given no further information about the little girl's condition. Jesus told the woman that he had primarily been sent by God, his Father, to meet the needs of Jewish people ('the children') and that she was not a Jew. 'First let the children eat all they want ... for it is not right to take the children's bread and toss it to the dogs.'

The woman, though, persisted with the conversation. She told Jesus that even dogs sometimes ate the leftovers - pieces of bread which were sometimes used to wipe the fingers after a meal and then thrown to the family pets. The normal word for 'dog' was used as a term of abuse for Gentiles but Jesus here uses the more affectionate word meaning a puppy or a pet. The woman clearly did not take offence at the words of Jesus although they do sound rather harsh to our ears.

Clearly it was the woman's faith which gave her the strength to pursue the conversation and led to the healing of her daughter. The implication is that Jesus was really putting that faith to the test and that the woman, through her perseverance, passed that test. The woman was told to return home where she would find that Jesus had cured the girl. This was, of course, an unusual feature of this miracle since Jesus usually came into direct physical contact with those people he healed.

Jesus and the Jews

Behind the story of the curing of the Syro-Phoenician woman's daughter there is a much more important sub-plot. From reading Mark's Gospel through carefully it seems that Jesus did largely restrict his message and ministry to Jewish listeners. He saw the main reason for his ministry in restoring members of the nation of Israel, the Jews, to their faith in God. At the same time, however, Jesus often commented that his Jewish listeners, including his own disciples, exhibited a marked lack of faith in him and his message.

The woman here responded to Jesus in a way that his disciples, on more than one occasion, failed to do. It is also noteworthy that a woman shows the faith that the men around her failed to find. She provided the necessary ingredients for a miracle to take place - and in that situation it did not matter whether she was a Jew or a Greek, male or female. Faith is faith no matter where it is found and who shows it.

Key Points

1 The miracle of Jesus healing the daughter of a Syro-Phoenician woman raises the question of the relationship between Judaism and non-Jews in the Gospels .
2 The woman's faith in the ability of Jesus to heal is the deciding factor. This faith is stronger than that shown by many Jews, even Jesus' own disciples.

Jesus rewarded the Syro-Phoenician woman for her faith in him, which was shown through her persistence.

Work to do

1 Choose two miracles in Mark's Gospel in which the faith of someone appears to be crucial.
   a Describe each of the miracles.
   b Who was called upon to show faith in both instances?
   c What did Jesus say which showed how important that faith was?
2 Jesus appears to be very harsh in his conversation with the Syro-Phoenician woman. How would you explain this?

In the Glossary

Disciple • Gentile

2.10 Jesus, the Messiah

Key Question

What kind of Messiah did their Scriptures lead the Jews to expect, and what kind of Messiah was Jesus?

The word 'Messiah' comes from the Hebrew language and refers to someone who is anointed with oil by a priest or prophet and is then sent out by God to perform a special task. It was often used by Jews to refer to the special king they were praying for who would deliver them from all their enemies before setting up God's kingdom on earth. They thought that this king would be descended from the Old Testament King David, the second king of Israel from the 10th century BCE, who was considered by Jews to have been their perfect leader.

The titles 'Messiah' and 'Christ'

Mark wrote his Gospel in Greek and used the Greek title 'Christ' frequently as well as the Hebrew word 'Messiah' to refer to Jesus. In fact, they mean the same thing: 'the anointed one'. Here are some examples of their use in Mark's Gospel:

a Mark opened his Gospel with the words: 'This is the Good News about Jesus Christ, the Son of God' (1.1).

b Asked by Jesus at Caesarea Philippi what the disciples thought of him, Peter answered: 'You are the Messiah' (8.29).

c Outside the city of Jerusalem blind Bartimaeus called out to Jesus and addressed him as 'the Son of David', meaning 'Christ' or 'king' (10.47).

d The people of Jerusalem recognised Jesus as the Messiah when they spread their coats and palm leaves on the road, crying: 'Praise God! God bless him who comes in the name of the Lord! God bless the coming kingdom of King David, our father!' (11.9–10).

e Both the High Priest (14.61) and Pontius Pilate (15.2) asked Jesus whether he was the Messiah.

f The notice placed above the head of Jesus on the cross by Pontius Pilate read 'The King of the Jews' (15.26), whilst the chief priests and teachers of the Law taunted 'the Messiah, the king of Israel' to come down from the cross and save himself (15.32).

What sort of Messiah was Jesus?

It soon became clear, however, that Jesus was not going to be the kind of Messiah that the Jews had been expecting. They looked for a warrior-king to drive the Romans from Israel by divine force, but Jesus taught his followers to love their enemies and do good to those who hated them. The Jewish leaders expected their Messiah to live a totally holy life, and one separate from all unholy contact, but Jesus mixed freely with prostitutes and other outcasts. They expected the Messiah to uphold the whole Law of Moses, but Jesus suggested the Law was not enough by itself and should not act like a great weight around people's necks. Little wonder, then, that the religious leaders and ordinary Jews were mystified by Jesus of Nazareth.

Pontius Pilate, the Roman governor, placed a title above the head of Jesus on the cross which read, 'Jesus of Nazareth. The King of the Jews'.

The prophet Isaiah, in the Old Testament, pictured animals who were natural enemies lying down next to each other when the Messiah came. The Messiah would bring a kingdom of peace into the world.

Largely because of this misunderstanding, Jesus was reluctant to accept the title of Messiah. In fact he made only one open admission of it in the whole of Mark's Gospel – at his trial (14.62). He was much more concerned with the Kingdom of God which he had come to introduce (see Unit 4) than his own Messiahship. He did not want to attract large crowds of people for the wrong reasons. He wanted to educate the people into seeing that he was a new kind of Messiah who:

a had been sent by God but was more than a mere messenger – he was God's Son;

b carried out his work by suffering and dying for others – not by using force;

c offered freedom to all – not from a foreign power but from the power of sin. Moreover, this freedom was not just for the Jews but for everyone – Jew and Gentile alike.

Key Points

1 The Messiah was a deliverer who, Jews were promised, would deliver them from their enemies. The Messiah would set up God's kingdom on earth.

2 Mark often used the title 'Christ' ('anointed one', 'Messiah') to refer to Jesus. The title 'Son of David' was also a Messianic title.

3 Jesus did not want to be publicly recognised as the Messiah because of the way people understood this role – as a military leader. Jesus had come to introduce God's kingdom: he was a spiritual and not a political leader.

Work to do

1 Write two sentences about each of the following:
   a King David;
   b the Messiah.
2 Describe two places in Mark's Gospel where someone recognised Jesus to be the Messiah.
3 Why do you think that Jesus tried to keep his Messiahship a secret for so long?
4 a Describe what kind of Messiah Jesus believed himself to be.
   b Explain two ways in which Jesus saw his role as Messiah differing from the figure that the Jews were expecting.

In the Glossary

Christ • Gentile • Gospel • High Priest • Jerusalem • Kingdom of God • Mark • Messiah • Moses • Peter • Pontius Pilate

2.11 At Caesarea Philippi

Read

Mark 8.27–30

Key Question

Why was the conversation that Jesus had with his disciples at Caesarea Philippi so important?

Caesarea Philippi was an inland city on the River Jordan at the foot of Mount Hermon. Herod the Great built a great temple there to the honour of Caesar Augustus, who had given the city to him. The city was named after the emperor by Herod's son, Philip the Tetrarch, who added his own name to distinguish it from the city of the same name on the Mediterranean coast. A grotto or shrine to the Greek god Pan stood near by, and the place became an important centre of emperor worship.

Jesus' questions at Caesarea Philippi

Situated on the very edge of Jewish territory, Caesarea Philippi was a quiet location where Jesus could preach in the villages without being mobbed by people seeking to be healed. On his way to the villages near to Caesarea Philippi, Jesus asked his disciples two questions.

1 "Tell me, who do people say I am?" (8.27)

It was very unusual for a rabbi to ask his disciples a question (it was always the other way round), but Jesus wanted his closest friends to understand more about him. The answers they gave were the same as those provided by Herod Antipas and the people before John the Baptist was beheaded (6.14–29) – that Jesus was John the Baptist, Elijah or one of the prophets. Opinions about Jesus had clearly not changed since the early stages of his ministry. Jews considered Elijah to be the greatest of the Old Testament prophets who, they believed, would return to earth before the Messiah came. Jesus equated him with John the Baptist (9.13) who had prepared the people for his own coming.

2 "What about you … Who do you say I am?" (8.29)

Jesus invited his disciples to go much further in their assessment of him. He was forcing them to make a judgement based on their own experience of him. On this occasion, as

on many others in Mark's Gospel, Peter acted as spokesman for the disciples. Whilst expressing his own personal opinion, he was also giving voice to the opinion of the other disciples. 'You are the Messiah' was his answer, and this is often referred to as Peter's confession (statement of faith). On the lips of Peter this confession clearly indicated that Jesus was believed by the disciples to be the long-awaited Messiah who would restore the fortunes of Israel and its supremacy over the world. It is the first time that any of the disciples had made such an open commitment to Jesus in Mark's Gospel.

St Peter's confession of faith in Jesus as the Messiah at Caesarea Philippi is a turning-point in Mark's Gospel.

The Messianic secret

This brings us to an important mystery in Mark's Gospel. For Mark this declaration of Peter, his main source of information, was the turning-point in his story. Part of the truth about Jesus was out, and from this moment onwards events in the Gospel move rapidly towards his death in Jerusalem. Yet, strangely, Jesus attempts to prevent the disciples from making their great discovery about him more widely known. He ordered his disciples at Caesarea Philippi not to tell anyone else and to keep the truth to themselves.

This is called the 'Messianic secret'. Why did Jesus go to great lengths to keep his real identity hidden? He certainly did not suggest that Peter was wrong or mistaken in his assessment. Rather, it was the people beyond his immediate circle of friends who concerned him most. He knew that they would not understand what kind of Messiah he was. They might even crown him as their king, to lead them in an uprising against the Romans, and that was something that Jesus did not want at any price. The people needed to be properly educated before they could be trusted with this news.

As we discover in the verses that follow (8.31–39), even Peter did not really understand what he was saying. He still had in mind a Messiah who would defeat the enemies of Israel – a far cry from the suffering and dying figure that Jesus was to become. He was to be a patient, humble, loving Messiah – the Suffering Servant as pictured in Isaiah 53. It was to be a long time before the disciples really understood that.

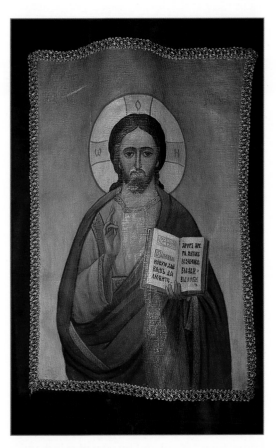

Jesus often told people, including some he had healed, not to speak about him to others. He didn't want them to get the wrong idea about his work.

Key Points

1 At Caesarea Philippi Jesus asked his disciples who they thought he was. Peter replied that Jesus was the Messiah – the first open declaration of this by any of the disciples.
2 Jesus was keen to keep this declaration quiet in Mark's Gospel – the so-called Messianic secret. He did not want the people to get any false ideas about him.
3 Peter did not understand what he was saying about Jesus. Jesus told Peter that only God could have revealed this to him.

Work to do

1 There are many references in the Old Testament to the coming of God's Messiah. Here are two of them:
   • Isaiah 11.1–2;
   • Isaiah 42.1–4.
   a Make a list in your book of the different things that these verses say about the coming Messiah.
   b Do they seem to present an accurate picture of the kind of person that Jesus was?
2 a What did Peter say that he believed about Jesus at Caesarea Philippi?
   b This incident has been called a 'watershed' in Mark's Gospel. What do you think this means?
   c What do you think is the importance of the conversation at Caesarea Philippi, both for Mark and for Christians today?

In the Glossary

Disciple • Elijah • Gospel • Herod Antipas • Herod the Great • Jerusalem • John the Baptist • Mark • Messiah • Old Testament • Peter • Prophet • Rabbi

2.12 Healing blind Bartimaeus

Read

Mark
10.46–52

Key Question

What is the importance of the story of Jesus healing blind Bartimaeus?

This is the last miracle recorded in Mark's Gospel, and the evangelist sets it very carefully in its context. Jesus was just leaving Jericho and travelling towards Jerusalem, about 15 miles away, when he came across a blind beggar, Bartimaeus, sitting by the roadside asking for alms and food from the people. The crowd following Jesus and his disciples were probably Galileans travelling to Jerusalem for the Passover festival during which Jesus was put to death.

In describing what happened to Bartimaeus, Mark is making an appeal to his readers to become followers of Jesus. He draws a parallel between the physical blindness of Bartimaeus and the spiritual blindness of his disciples (10.35–45). The message for Christians today is that it is only through faith in Jesus that they can grow in their knowledge of God and receive physical and spiritual healing.

The miracle

There are several important things to notice in the story of the healing of blind Bartimaeus as it unfolds: the title 'Son of David' used by the blind man to refer to Jesus; the faith of the blind man; and the theme of discipleship.

The Son of David

Bartimaeus cried out: 'Jesus! Son of David! Take pity on me!' (10.47). For centuries Jews had expected that their Messiah would be a descendant of King David, Israel's ideal ruler, as we saw in Unit 2.10. David, Israel's second king, had ruled from 1010 to 970 BCE. During his reign he had captured Jerusalem and made it his capital city, ushering in the 'golden age' to which all Jews looked back with nostalgia. For a short time Israel was safe from any outside threat as the Philistines, the greatest threat to their safety, were defeated.

The approval of God clearly rested on David. He had been promised by God that one of his descendants would always occupy the throne, and that is why the Messiah was

called 'the Son of David'. Both Matthew and Luke, in their Gospels, traced the family-tree of Jesus back to David through Joseph, his father, and beyond (Matthew 1.1–17; Luke 3.23–37). In Mark, though, the title 'Son of David' is only used twice – here and in 12.35–37.

The faith of the blind man

The faith of Bartimaeus in Jesus to heal him was tested when the crowd tried to prevent him calling out for help. Jesus responded by calling for Bartimaeus to come to him, and Mark captured the excitement of the moment when he described what happened next:

> "He threw off his cloak, jumped up, and came to Jesus."
> (10.50)

Jesus immediately tested the man's faith by asking him what he most wanted.

> "'Teacher,' the blind man answered, 'I want to see again.' 'Go,' Jesus told him, 'your faith has made you well.'"
> (10.51–52)

This reminds us of the words that Jesus had already spoken to the woman with the haemorrhage:

> "My daughter, your faith has made you well. Go in peace and be healed of your trouble."
> (5.34)

The theme of discipleship

The theme of discipleship becomes prominent in the second half of Mark's Gospel. The cure of the man was instantaneous. It was Bartimaeus' willingness to act on his belief that Jesus was the Messiah that healed him. The same truth, though, was still hidden from the disciples, who remained spiritually blind.

The value of the miracle

The words that end Mark's description of the healing of Bartimaeus may well have a coded message in them. He tells us that the blind man was able to see and 'followed Jesus on the road [way]' (10.52). It was the work of the disciples to follow Jesus on the road – and that road eventually led to Jerusalem and death. Every Christian is, likewise, called to follow Jesus to the end – if necessary, to death. The early Christians are often called 'followers of the Way'.

For your Information

The title 'Son of David' came from the Old Testament and underlined the fact that Jesus was God's Messiah. Here are some of the references:

● Old Testament: Jeremiah 23.5; Ezekiel 34.23-24; Isaiah 16.5;

● New Testament: Matthew 12.23; 15.22; 20.30; 21.29; Mark 10.47–48; 12.35–37; Luke 18.35–37; John 7.41–42.

Key Points

1 The healing of blind Bartimaeus is the last miracle in Mark's Gospel.
2 Mark draws a parallel between the spiritual blindness of the disciples and the restoration of physical sight to Bartimaeus.
3 By calling Jesus 'Son of David' Bartimaeus recognised Jesus as the Messiah – an insight denied to the disciples.
4 It was the faith of Bartimaeus that made it possible for Jesus to heal him.

Work to do

1 a Where was Jesus when he met Bartimaeus, and where was the blind beggar?
  b What was the significance of Bartimaeus calling Jesus 'the Son of David'? On which other occasion was this title applied to Jesus in Mark's Gospel?
  c What was Mark possibly trying to say when he noted that Bartimaeus 'followed Jesus on the road' after his blindness had been cured?

2 Bartimaeus was blind. He desperately wanted to see. Why do you think that Jesus asked him what he wanted most?
3 a Tell the story of Bartimaeus in your own words.
  b What message do you think Mark was trying to convey through the story?

In the Glossary

Disciple • Gospel • Jerusalem • Luke • Mark • Matthew • Messiah • Passover

Although the disciples deserted Jesus at the end, there were some women followers who stayed with him – as this Station of the Cross reminds us.

2.13 Jesus enters Jerusalem

Read

Mark
11.1–25

Key Question

What was the significance of the dramatic way in which Jesus entered Jerusalem on Palm Sunday, and what happened afterwards?

A few days before he was crucified Jesus arrived in Jerusalem with his disciples, just as the city was filling up with Jewish pilgrims arriving for the Passover festival. Tension was always high at this time of the year because, at this festival, Jews looked back to the time when God delivered their ancestors under Moses from Egyptian slavery. Every Jew hoped that God would work another miracle for them by sending the long-awaited Messiah and breaking the stranglehold of the Romans over them. They were sure that God could not ignore their cries for help much longer.

The arrival of the Messiah

Mark's description of the entry of Jesus into Jerusalem shows us that Jesus did nothing to dampen down these hopes. In fact, the arrival of Jesus on a donkey in the city only heightened them. Jesus rode into Jerusalem as King David and King Solomon might have entered their capital centuries earlier, with branches and clothes spread on the road in front of them. Today, in many developing countries, palm and banana leaves are often spread in a similar way to greet important visitors to village festivals.

The way that the people danced in the streets when Jesus entered the city (11.9) suggests that they believed that their Messiah had arrived. Mark must have had in mind the Old Testament prophecy:

> "Rejoice, rejoice, people of Zion
> [Jerusalem]!
>   Shout for joy, you people of Jerusalem!
>   Look, your king is coming to you!
> He comes triumphant and victorious,
>   but humble and riding on a donkey –
>   on a colt, the foal of a donkey."
>   (Zechariah 9.9)

Each year many Christians re-enact this event on Palm Sunday when they hold processions and carry palm leaves or crosses through the streets. It heralds the start of Holy Week which ends with Easter Saturday.

Two further actions of Jesus followed soon after his dramatic entry into the city: the cleansing of the Temple, and the cursing of the fig-tree.

The cleansing of the Temple

The first Temple in Jerusalem had been built by King Solomon in the 10th century BCE, but this was destroyed in 587 BCE. The present building was put up by the much-hated Herod the Great in an attempt to make himself popular with the Jews. The outer courtyard, the Court of the Gentiles, was the only part of the complex open to both Jews and Gentiles. This part, the area that Jesus cleansed, was used for two main activities – to sell animals that were used for sacrifice in the Temple, and to change money. Roman coinage, carrying the head of the emperor, was never used in the Temple. The Jews had to change them for old Hebrew coins and the cost of doing this was very high.

The money-changers and those who sold animals made vast profits. Jesus stopped the commerce by overturning their tables. Taking place in the Court of the Gentiles, this was a reminder that God cared as deeply for the Gentiles as for the Jews. It is, though, the anger and violence that Jesus showed

A modern Palm Sunday procession celebrating the entry of Jesus into Jerusalem as the Messiah.

Jesus encouraged people to have faith in God and to expect him to answer their prayers.

which surprises many people. Jesus often used 'verbal violence' against his opponents, but this is the only time in the Gospels that he used physical violence. The significance of his action, though, would have been apparent to the religious leaders and other Jews. They knew only too well that cleansing the Temple was one of the first actions that the Messiah was traditionally expected to carry out.

Key Points

1 The entry of Jesus into Jerusalem on a donkey was the entry of the Messiah. Both his disciples and the people in the crowd recognised him as such.

2 Jesus did nothing at the time to dampen down the hopes of the people or of his disciples.

3 Jesus cleansed the Temple of those who had turned it into a place of commerce rather than prayer. This is the only recorded instance of Jesus using violence.

Work to do

1 "Praise God! God bless him who comes in the name of the Lord! God bless the coming kingdom of King David, our father! Praise God!"
(11.9–10)

  a Who said these words?
  b What was the occasion?
  c What did the people of Jerusalem think when they saw Jesus riding into their city on a donkey?
  d This action of Jesus has been called 'an acted parable'. What do you think this description means?
  e What was Jesus trying to teach his disciples and the crowd through his actions?

2 a Outline Mark's account of the cleansing of the Temple in Jerusalem.
  b Explain carefully what is surprising about this incident, and how it could possibly be explained.

In the Glossary

Disciple • Easter • Gentiles • Herod the Great • Holy Week • Jerusalem • Mark • Messiah • Old Testament • Palm Sunday • Parable • Passover • Temple

Read

Mark
14.32–52

Key Question

Why was the experience in the Garden of Gethsemane so distressing for Jesus?

The experience in the Garden of Gethsemane was the most shattering in the life of Jesus. He chose to share it with the same group of friends – Peter, James and John – who had shared other experiences, such as the Transfiguration, with him in the past. For them, too, it was a great test of character, but they were unable to provide the support that Jesus needed.

In the garden

Jesus went straight from sharing his last meal with his disciples (see Unit 8.1) to the Garden of Gethsemane (see photograph) on the slopes of the Mount of Olives. Jesus was aware that his opponents were closing in on him, and that he had little time left. It was only human and natural that he should dread what lay ahead of him. He told his friends:

> "The sorrow in my heart is so great that it almost crushes me."
> (14.34)

At no other time in Mark's Gospel is the humanity of Jesus so apparent. He left his disciples and went ahead of them to pray alone three times. Each time, after praying, he returned to find them sleeping. While he was away from them he prayed in

desperation to his Father that, even at this late hour, he might be spared the suffering that lay ahead of him:

> "Father … my Father! All things are possible for you. Take this cup of suffering away from me. Yet not what I want, but what you want."
> (14.36)

From this description of the suffering of Jesus two clear themes emerge:

1 Despite his dread of what lay ahead, Jesus remained faithful to God – although God seemed to have deserted him. Mark does not underplay the cost of this obedience to Jesus. We are made painfully aware of the loneliness and torment through which he passed. Up to the very last moment Jesus hoped that there might be some way out – but there wasn't.

2 The disciples failed to appreciate the seriousness of the time through which Jesus was passing – they could not even stay awake. We have come across the failure of the disciples to support Jesus many times before, and the reader of the Gospel is hardly surprised when it happens again here.

A small sculpture placed at the entrance to the Garden of Gethsemane reminds visitors of what happened there a long time ago.

The arrest of Jesus

Finally, Jesus accepted that his hour had come. The crowd, led by Judas Iscariot, approached. Turning to his three disciples, Jesus told them:

> "Get up, let us go. Look, here is the man who is betraying me!"
> (14.42)

The crowd from the Sanhedrin ('sent by the chief priests, the teachers of the Law and the elders') arrived with Judas at their head. For many months the twelve disciples had shared their lives with Jesus, but now one of them was to hand Jesus over to his enemies. To Mark, and his Christian readers, this was the ultimate betrayal. This is highlighted when Judas approached Jesus, kissed him and respectfully called him 'rabbi'. The kiss, a sign of love and respect, became the final act of a betrayer. Shortly afterwards, we discover from Matthew's Gospel, Judas committed suicide.

Jesus was not arrested without a protest. He complained of being treated like a common criminal, arrested by men carrying swords and staves. The rebuke stung the religious authorities. They had already decided to arrest Jesus in the middle of the night in case the people objected (12.12). Now, with the Passover festival about to start in a few hours, they had to move quickly.

Key Points

1 His experience in the Garden of Gethsemane was the most spiritually disturbing in the life of Jesus. He knew that intense suffering was at hand and felt that God had deserted him.
2 Although Jesus wanted to share this experience with Peter, James and John, they failed to support him. They could not stay awake.
3 After much prayer Jesus came to accept that God's will for him involved suffering.
4 Jesus was arrested directly after the Gethsemane experience. Judas, one of his disciples, led the party of soldiers and religious leaders.

Work to do

1 "Are you still sleeping and resting? Enough! The hour has come! Look, the Son of Man is now being handed over to the power of sinful men." (14.41)
   a Why did Jesus spend his last few hours of freedom in the Garden of Gethsemane, and who did he take with him?
   b What insights does Mark give us about the state of mind of Jesus at the time?
   c What indications are there in Mark's account to show that Jesus knew that the end of his life was close?
2 The experience in the garden was only shared by three of his disciples. Describe briefly two other occasions when the same disciples shared important experiences with Jesus.
3 "Did you have to come with swords and clubs to capture me, as though I were an outlaw?" (14.48)
   a Who was Jesus speaking to?
   b What was the occasion for these words?
   c What part did Judas play in the arrest of Jesus?
   d Why did Jesus express his surprise when a group of armed soldiers arrived to arrest him?
4 a Describe the scene in the Garden of Gethsemane before Jesus was arrested by the Temple guards.
   b Do you think that Mark's account is a historically accurate description of what is likely to have taken place?
5 Describe the events of Holy Week in Mark's Gospel, from Palm Sunday through to the arrest of Jesus.

In the Glossary

Disciple • Gospel • James • John • Judas Iscariot • Mark • Passover • Peter • Rabbi • Sanhedrin • Transfiguration

3.2 The Jewish trial and Peter's denial

Read

Mark 14.53–72

Key Question

What was the significance of the trial of Jesus before the Sanhedrin, and of Peter's denial?

Mark describes two trials of Jesus. The first of these took place before the 70 members of the Sanhedrin (the Jewish Council), people with considerable influence in the Jewish community. In its haste to condemn Jesus to death the Sanhedrin, by meeting late at night, was breaking its own rules since:

a The Sanhedrin was only allowed to gather together in daylight hours, and it could not meet in the house of the High Priest.

b Any sentence of death required confirmation by another sitting of the Sanhedrin within 24 hours of the first. In the case of Jesus, this second sitting did not take place.

c No hearing involving the death penalty could take place on the eve of the Sabbath day or any feast day. On this occasion, though, the following day was the Sabbath, and the night of the hearing was the beginning of the Passover festival.

The trial

In Mark's description of the trial of Jesus before the Jewish court, the events fall into three parts: the search for evidence, questioning from the High Priest and the reaction of the Jewish leaders.

According to its own laws, the Sanhedrin had to find two independent witnesses who could give identical evidence when out of earshot of each other. Mark tells us:

> "Many witnesses told lies against Jesus, but their stories did not agree."
> (Mark 14.56)

Some witnesses testified that Jesus had prophesied that the Temple would be destroyed and then rebuilt within three days. This accusation was probably based on an incident recorded earlier by Mark (13.1–2). Even here, though, the witnesses did not agree. The High Priest asked Jesus:

"'Have you no answer to the accusation they bring against you?' But Jesus kept quiet and would not say a word. Again the High Priest questioned him, 'Are you the Messiah, the Son of the Blessed God?'" (14.60–61)

Elsewhere in Mark's Gospel Jesus avoided the title of Messiah, but not here.

The claim of Jesus was, to Jewish ears, blasphemy. Any Jew who heard a blasphemous statement tore his clothes. That is what the High Priest did, and the Sanhedrin unanimously condemned Jesus to death.

To Christians undergoing persecution, the message was one of encouragement. They knew that their own persecution was unjust and unfair. If Christ endured his sufferings, though, they could do the same with God's help.

The denial of Peter

Peter, alone amongst the disciples, tried to stay in touch with Jesus. He followed the crowd to the house of the High Priest where the Sanhedrin was meeting. He sat to warm himself in the courtyard of the house, where he was challenged on two occasions. First, a servant girl challenged him as a companion of Jesus. Peter denied it totally and the cock crowed for the first time. Peter tried to merge into the crowd but the same girl challenged him a second time. Again he denied it strongly. By now the crowd had detected his Galilean accent and challenged him a third time. Peter denied it vehemently and the cock crowed again.

Jesus had already prophesied that Peter would deny him (14.29–31) and the cock crowing a second time brought these words back to Peter. Mark described his subsequent collapse dramatically:

> "And he broke down and cried."
> (14.72)

The story of Peter's denial is found in all four Gospels. Yet, by the time that Mark was writing, Peter had been crucified for his faith in Christ. Peter was greatly respected as one of the first Christian martyrs. The incident was included to show that everyone, including great leaders, sometimes failed and needed the forgiveness of God. The Christians were suffering great persecution at the time that Mark was writing, so this was a very encouraging message.

Key Points

1 After the arrest of Jesus his first trial took place before the Sanhedrin, the Jewish Council. The witnesses could not agree on their evidence against him.
2 Peter denied that he had ever known Jesus when he was challenged. He did so three times, as Jesus had prophesied.
3 Peter was desperately upset by what he had done. He became a great Christian leader and one of the first Christian martyrs.

Work to do

1 a Where did the first trial of Jesus take place?
  b Who tried him?
  c What false evidence was given against him?
  d What did the High Priest ask Jesus, and how did he reply?
  e Why did the High Priest tear his robes, and what did that indicate?
  f What punishment was thought fitting for the 'crime' of Jesus?
2 According to Mark, Peter followed Jesus at a distance after he had been arrested, but the other disciples were nowhere to be seen. What conclusion do you think Mark might have been inviting his readers to draw from this?
3 a Tell the story of Peter's denial in your own words.
  b Why do you think that Mark saw this event as being very important – for Jesus, for Peter and for the early Church?
4 Descibe, in your own words, the trial of Jesus before the Sanhedrin.

In the Glossary

Blasphemy • Gospel • High Priest • Mark • Messiah • Passover • Peter • Sabbath day • Sanhedrin • Temple

Jesus with his disciples at the Last Supper. Mark obtained most of his information for his Gospel from Peter – including, presumably, the story of his denial of Jesus.

3.3   The Roman trial

Read

**Mark
15.1–15**

**Key
Question**

**Why did
Pilate
condemn
Jesus to
death?**

The Sanhedrin (see Unit 3.2) had already found Jesus guilty of the crime of blasphemy. Although the Jewish law demanded the death penalty for this crime, it seems that, under the Romans, the Jews did not have the power to carry the sentence out. If Jesus was to be executed then he must be condemned by a Roman court as well. This can be the only reason why Jesus was brought before the political authorities, since the Romans are hardly mentioned in Mark's Gospel until this point. The time for approaching a senior Roman official was early in the morning, and this may explain why the Sanhedrin met late at night, against its own rules. The working day of a Roman gentleman began at dawn or even earlier. He would have finished his official duties by late morning.

The trial before Pilate

By the time that Jesus is taken before Pilate the charge has changed from that of the earlier trial. No mention is made of the religious crime of blasphemy, since that would have been of no interest to the Romans. Pilate would only execute Jesus if he thought that he represented a threat to the Roman Empire – and his own career. This is why the claim of Jesus to be the Messiah, the King, is uppermost in the trial before Pilate. A Messiah would offer the people an alternative to the power and authority of the emperor in Rome, and it was this possibility that greatly concerned Pontius Pilate. If the news reached Rome it would greatly concern his superiors as well. (You can find out more about Pontius Pilate in the information box.)

Pilate knew that he could not ignore Jesus. He tried to fall back on a custom which is mentioned by Mark but does not seem to have been mentioned anywhere else. There was a tradition for the Roman governor to release one prisoner, of the people's choice, each Passover. Pilate offered to release Jesus under this arrangement but, according to Mark, the offer was firmly refused by the crowd under incitement from the chief priests (15.11).

Instead, the crowd chose Barabbas. We know nothing about Barabbas outside the Gospels. From the Gospels we discover that he had been imprisoned either for robbery (John 18.40) or for leading an uprising and murder (Mark 15.7 and Luke 23.19). These crimes were common in the violent times in which Jesus lived in Palestine. In demanding the release of Barabbas the crowd were also

After condemning Jesus to death Pontius Pilate washed his hands, to suggest to the crowd that he was innocent of what was about to happen.

demanding the crucifixion of Jesus. They were encouraged in making this demand by the chief priests, who belonged to the upper class and had a great deal to lose by any uprising against the governing authorities that Jesus might have prompted. In their eyes he was better dead!

The role of the Jews

The record of the Jewish involvement in, and responsibility for, the death of Jesus in Mark, and in the other Gospels, has led throughout history to a very negative attitude being adopted by the Christian Church towards the Jewish people. This negative attitude, called antisemitism, has led throughout history to Christian mobs killing Jews to avenge the crucifixion of Jesus. Certainly the Gospels unfairly hold the Jews responsible for an act which could only have taken place if the Romans had taken the leading role. The Jews did not have the authority to play a decisive part in the death of Jesus.

The narrative ends with Pilate once again showing his weakness of character by releasing Barabbas because 'he wanted to please the crowd' (15.15). Having had Jesus whipped, he then handed him over to be crucified.

For your Information

Concerning Pontius Pilate we know that:

a he was the Roman prefect, later the procurator, in charge of the province of Judea between 26 and 36 CE;

b he greatly offended the Jews and is thought to have murdered many Galileans in one single incident;

c the New Testament accounts are much kinder to Pilate than the historical evidence supports. They present him as a weak man who wanted to let Jesus go, if he could find a way of doing so. This approach is understandable if one remembers that the Church had to exist, and live, in the Roman world for a long time after the death of Jesus. Mark certainly did not want to upset the Roman authorities. We do know, however, that Pilate was finally dismissed by the Roman emperor because he was too cruel!

Key Points

1 The Sanhedrin found Jesus guilty but only the Roman governor could authorise his execution.
2 At the Roman trial Jesus was charged with political, not religious, crimes – especially treason.
3 Pilate tried to use an old custom and release Jesus. The crowd chose Barabbas, a murderer, to be released instead.
4 Although Mark here blames the Jewish leaders for the death of Jesus it seems that most of the blame should fall on the Romans.

Work to do

1 a What did Pilate ask Jesus, and what was his reply?
  b Why did Pilate ask the crowd what he should do with Jesus?
  c Why did the crowd answer as it did?
  d Who was Barabbas?
  e How did the Roman soldiers treat Jesus?
2 Why was it important for Mark to imply that Pilate thought Jesus was innocent?
3 Retell Mark's accounts of the trials of Jesus before:
  a the Sanhedrin;
  b Pontius Pilate.
  What are the main similarities and differences between the accounts?
4 a What picture does Mark portray of Pontius Pilate?
  b What do we know about the kind of person that Pontius Pilate actually was?
  c Why do you think that these two pictures are so different?

In the Glossary

Blasphemy • Gospel • Mark • Messiah • Passover • Pontius Pilate • Sanhedrin

3.4   The crucifixion

Read

**Mark
15.21–41**

**Key
Question**

**What does
Mark tell us
about the
crucifixion
of Jesus?**

Normally, after the sentence of death had been passed in Jerusalem, the condemned man was expected to carry his own crossbeam to the place of execution. This was usually on a hill or mound so that the public execution could be seen by everyone and act as a deterrent to them. Jesus, weakened by persistent abuse and beating at the hands of the Roman soldiers, could not carry his own crossbeam and so a bystander, Simon of Cyrene, was forced to carry it for him.

This is one of the events from the closing hours of the life of Jesus that is portrayed in the fourteen Stations of the Cross which are to be found in every Catholic church (see photograph). The last journey of Jesus to the place of execution is still commemorated each week by Christians in Jerusalem. They follow the Stations of the Cross which have been placed along the Via Dolorosa ('the way of sorrow'), the traditional route that Jesus is believed to have taken to Calvary. Many pilgrims walk this route each year on Good Friday, the day on which Christians throughout the world remember the death of Jesus, to share the journey with him.

*Jesus was so
weakened by his
treatment at the
hands of the
Roman soldiers
that he needed
help to carry the
cross to the place
of execution.*

Crucifixion

Roman citizens, whatever their crime, were exempt from crucifixion since this was considered a shameful form of execution. Criminals were hung naked on the cross and exposed to the ridicule and jeers of those passing by. Because of Jewish modesty about the human body, however, their criminals were allowed to wear a loin-cloth.

The shape of the cross itself seems to have varied from place to place in the Roman Empire. Sometimes it was an upright stake, sometimes X-shaped and often T-shaped. The cross on which Jesus was crucified was probably an upright pole with a cross-bar. A stake was driven through the palms of the hands and the feet.

The death of Jesus

The crucifixion of Jesus took place at Golgotha, a Hebrew word meaning 'the place of the skull' ('Calvary' in Greek). The site is covered today with church buildings, although a nearby hill, sometimes called 'Gordon's Calvary', bears a strong resemblance to the shape of a skull. Mark's description of the crucifixion is the briefest and most direct of all four Gospel accounts. It focuses on the reactions of those who passed by as Jesus was dying: the soldiers, the chief priests and scribes, and the criminals executed with him.

The soldiers were cold and apathetic, simply carrying out a job of work. This crucifixion was no different to them than any other. It was customary for the soldiers to take all of the prisoners' clothing, and to throw dice to see who would take what. This is what they did at the foot of the cross of Jesus (15.24).

The chief priests and the teachers of the Law (the scribes) jeered at Jesus, saying:

> "He saved others, but he cannot save himself! Let us see the Messiah, the king of Israel, come down from the cross now, and we will believe in him!"
> (15.31–32)

The two criminals executed at the same time as Jesus threw insults at him. In Luke's account, one of the criminals repented and sought the forgiveness of Jesus (23.40–43) but there is no indication of this happening in Mark's account.

The crucifixion began, according to Mark's timing, at 9.00 a.m. The notice placed above his head giving the reason for his execution said 'The King of the Jews'. Pilate recognised that Jesus as a king, presented, a threat to the Roman Empire (although the inscription could simply have been an ironic comment by the Roman governor). At noon 'the whole country' was covered in a darkness that lasted for three hours. Then Jesus cried out in a loud voice:

> "'Eloi, Eloi, lema sabachthani?' which means, 'My God, my God, why did you abandon me?'"
> (15.34)

Shortly afterwards, with a loud cry, Jesus died. His death had taken a remarkably short time, as those being crucified often took a day or more to die. None of the disciples is mentioned by Mark as witnessing the last hour of Jesus, although some women, including Mary Magdalene, another Mary and Salome, are mentioned as watching from a distance. These women were to play a very important part in the events that followed (see Unit 3.6).

By calling Jesus a king on the inscription on his cross Pilate seems to imply that he did represent a political threat to the Roman Empire.

Key Points

1 The Stations of the Cross in every Catholic church show the important events in the last hours of the life of Jesus.
2 Crucifixion was a very cruel method of execution – the Romans would not crucify their own citizens.
3 At the end of his life Jesus suffered emotionally as well as physically. Onlookers and the two men who died alongside him mocked him.
4 For three hours before Jesus died there was total darkness over the earth. He died quickly. His last hours were witnessed by several women followers.

Work to do

1 Describe two ways in which Jesus suffered before he died.
2 a Who carried the cross for Jesus?
  b What was the place of execution called, and what did it mean?
  c At what time was Jesus crucified?
  d Who was crucified with Jesus?
  e What accusation was placed above the head of Jesus, and why?
3 Why do you think that Mark, in his account of the death of Jesus, concentrates on the reactions of the onlookers?

In the Glossary

Good Friday • Gospel • Jerusalem • Luke • Mark • Messiah • Pontius Pilate • Roman Catholic Church • Scribe • Stations of the Cross • Via Dolorosa

3.5 Why did Jesus die?

Key Question

How did the early Christians understand the reasons behind the death of Jesus?

The early Christians knew that Jesus had been put to death and were convinced that he had returned to life. These two events formed the cornerstone of their faith in God. They took them to be conclusive proof that Jesus was God's Messiah. This, though, presented them with a real problem. The Jewish Scriptures clearly said that anyone put to death was cursed by God and Jesus had been executed as a common criminal. How could this happen to the Messiah and how should they understand his death?

Understanding the death of Jesus

To solve the problem of the crucified Messiah the early Christians searched their collections of the sayings of Jesus. These collections had been put together long before the first Gospel had been written and were highly valued. They were circulated widely amongst the young churches. In them the early Christians found two kinds of sayings from Jesus about his forthcoming death.

1 Sayings in which Jesus predicted that he would be put to death by his enemies. Mark later included some of these sayings in his Gospel. Jesus clearly expected to suffer and die. On each occasion that Jesus spoke about this he referred to himself as the Son of Man. You can find an example of this in the information box.

2 Sayings in which Jesus said that his death would bring about a very important change in the relationship between God and the human race. Jesus had died during the Jewish festival of Passover. Passover was the most important Jewish festival because it celebrated the greatest event in Jewish history – the deliverance of the Jews from the Egyptians. It had taken a dramatic miracle to bring this about. Now, though, a much greater miracle was to take place. Jesus, by his death, would bring about the deliverance of everyone from their sins.

The death of Jesus as a sacrifice

The Jewish Scriptures offered another clue to understanding the death of Jesus. God had made a covenant (agreement) with the Jews in which he promised to be their God as long as they remained faithful to him in their worship. Part of this Jewish obligation was to offer animal sacrifices to God so that their sins could be forgiven. This took place each year on the Day of Atonement, the most solemn day of the year for all Jews.

The early Christians linked this with the death of Jesus. There were, though, crucial differences. The sacrifice of an animal could only take away some sins and it needed to be repeated continually. The death of Jesus took away all sins and it was a once-and-for-all sacrifice. It made possible a new covenant between God and the human race:

"This is my blood which is poured out for many, my blood which seals God's covenant."
(14.24)

It took the Christian Church over 400 years before it could use the cross as a symbol of the Christian faith.

The idea that the death of Jesus put everything right between God and human beings is called the 'atonement' (at-one-ment).

For your Information

Mark records these words of Jesus:

"The Son of Man did not come to be served, but to serve, and to give his life a ransom for many."
(10.45)

Key Points

1 Jesus taught that his death was inevitable – and would introduce a new relationship between God and the human race.
2 The death of Jesus was a sacrifice, replacing the old animal sacrifices, which would secure the forgiveness of sins.
3 The death of Jesus put everything right between God and human beings – it was an 'atonement'.

Work to do

1 a Jesus died during a Jewish festival. What was the name of the festival?
   b What did Jews remember and celebrate during this festival?
2 Why was the death of Jesus as a common criminal a problem for the early Christians?
3 What does the word 'atonement' mean and what does it have to do with the death of Jesus?
4 Read the words of Jesus in the information box. What do you think they tell us about the death of Jesus?

In the Glossary

Messiah • Passover • Son of Man

The early Christians fell back on the Jewish Scriptures to understand the death of Jesus.

3.6   Burial and resurrection

Read

Mark
15.42–16.8

Key Question

What does Mark tell us about the burial and resurrection of Jesus?

It is not easy to follow Mark's chronology precisely. It seems that Jesus died just before sunset on the Friday afternoon. He was buried in great haste just before the Sabbath day started. Then, after spending Saturday in the tomb, he returned to life early on the Sunday morning.

The burial of Jesus

The burial story was very important for Mark, and his Christian readers, as it emphasised that Jesus had really died. Mark is careful to tell us that Pilate checked that Jesus was dead before releasing his body to Joseph of Arimathea, a wealthy Jew. Joseph was a prominent member of the Sanhedrin and a loyal Pharisee 'who was waiting for the coming of the Kingdom of God'.

As an orthodox Jew, Joseph would have shared the usual Jewish scruples about coming into contact with a dead body, especially that of a 'criminal' which was regarded as 'unclean'. Under Roman law a person executed for treason, as Jesus was, was not buried. The body was left on the cross to be picked clean by scavenging birds. Jesus, however, was a Jew and Jewish tradition determined that everyone should be buried – even criminals. The Jews also insisted that no body should be left on a cross after the Sabbath day had started.

Perhaps Joseph was simply acting like a good Jew and taking care of those unable to look after themselves. Alternatively, he may have been a secret Jewish disciple who had been devastated by the death of Jesus and determined to give him a decent burial. Either way, he laid the body of Jesus in his own, unused tomb.

The resurrection of Jesus

Bodies were anointed with oils and spices directly after death to preserve them for as long as possible. Jesus had died, however, just before the Sabbath day was about to begin, and so such work, the responsibility of women, could not take place. The women who visited the tomb 24 hours later, not only came to anoint the body but also to fulfil a Jewish duty to visit the grave of someone who had died for three days after burial. The

same three women are mentioned – Mary Magdalene, Mary, the mother of James, and Salome – who observed the death of Jesus from a distance (see Unit 3.4).

Throughout his Gospel Mark is reluctant to speak of the 'supernatural' such as angels, and he maintains this reluctance here. It is a 'young man' who met the three women when they visited the tomb early on the Sunday morning. He was clearly an angel, though, since he was dressed in white and was responsible for rolling the large stone away from the mouth of the tomb. This is a miracle, but the mechanics of what happened do not interest Mark. He does not provide any important information about it. Instead, the significance of the event for Mark, and the early Church, can be found in the angel's words:

> "Don't be alarmed … I know you are looking for Jesus of Nazareth, who was crucified. He is not here – he has been raised! Look, here is the place where they put him."
> (16.6)

Mark seems to have been reluctant to identify the person at the tomb as an angel.

The angel tells the women to pass this information on to the disciples – and to Peter. This reminds us of the recent denial of Peter (see Unit 3.2) as well as underlining the great respect which he was given in the early Church. Mark was probably writing around the time that Peter was put to death by the Roman emperor Nero for his faith in Christ. So, for Peter and all the disciples, the death of Jesus was not the end of the story. As Mark knew, the very disciples who had forsaken Jesus at the time of his greatest need were to become the founding members of the Christian Church.

For your Information

Where did Mark end his Gospel? Although you will find an ending which includes Jesus appearing several times to his disciples, this almost certainly did not come from Mark. All of the early manuscripts that we have end with the women running from the tomb, too frightened to tell anyone what they have seen. If that is the real end of Mark's Gospel then it leads us to wonder:

a whether Mark intended to finish his Gospel at this point;

b whether Mark met a sudden death which prevented him from finishing his Gospel;

c whether Mark did write another ending which has been lost.

Key Points

1 For Mark, the burial story showed that Jesus had really died.
2 The body of Jesus was placed in the unused tomb of Joseph of Arimathea. Jews had very strict rules about handling a dead body – especially that of a condemned criminal.
3 The angel in the tomb is only seen by the women. They go on to tell the disciples.
4 The ending of Mark's Gospel is very abrupt. The real ending has probably been lost.
5 The resurrection of Jesus is the most important Christian belief.

Work to do

1 Describe the arrangements that were made, according to Mark, to bury the body of Jesus.
2 a Name the women who were watching from a distance when Jesus died.
   b Who asked Pilate for the body of Jesus? Why do you think he did this?
   c What was done with the body of Jesus?
3 a What two reasons does Mark give for the visit of the women to the tomb of Jesus?
   b What did they find when they arrived?
   c Why is the resurrection of Jesus so important for Christian faith?

For Mark, the resurrection proved that the death of Jesus was not the end of the story. This was a message of hope for Peter and the disciples.

In the Glossary

Angel • Disciple • Gospel • Kingdom of God • Mark • Pharisees • Pontius Pilate • Sabbath day • Sanhedrin

3.7 Resurrection appearances and the Commission

Read

Mark 16.9–20

**Key Question**

What does the 'longer ending' to Mark's Gospel tell us about Jesus after he rose from the dead?

Mark's Gospel almost certainly ends at 16.8. Another ending (16.9–20), however, was attached to the Gospel at an early stage, although we do not know who wrote it. This is called the 'longer ending' because just verses 9 and 10 were also attached to the Gospel at some time. In the longer ending verses 9–14 refer to three occasions when Jesus appeared to different people after his resurrection.

The longer ending

The so-called 'longer ending' to Mark's Gospel may originally have been a document which was used to teach new converts about Christianity. Clearly the resurrection of Jesus was a very important topic which was covered in special instruction classes for those new to the Christian faith. It may have been put together from extracts taken from the other Gospels. It briefly mentions the appearances of Jesus to:

- Mary Magdalene;
- two travellers;
- the eleven disciples.

All of these references are paralleled by references in Matthew, Luke or John.

The Commission

The risen Jesus tells those that he appears to that they are to preach the Gospel. This is called the Commission. He also informed them that they would have the power to drive out demons, heal people, speak in strange languages, pick up snakes and drink poison without being harmed. All of these powers, except the drinking of poison, are mentioned in the Acts of the Apostles as being seen in the ministry of the disciples.

Many Christians, however, feel that some of these activities are rather bizarre, such as handling poisonous snakes and drinking poison. They maintain that such activities may well have been carried out by a group in the 2nd century which had strayed from the original teachings of Jesus. Others maintain that they are not a description of how

Christians should behave but just a figurative way of saying that there is nothing that Christians cannot do, as long as they trust God.

After his resurrection Jesus is said to have stayed on earth a further forty days, appearing to different groups of people.

TO THE GLORY OF GOD
ELLEN CARTWRIGHT

AND IN LOVING MEMOR
AT REST 2ND FEB. 1

The ascension

After his appearance to his disciples Jesus is taken up into heaven. Although some Christians celebrate Ascension Day forty days after Easter, most do not take the ascension of Jesus into 'heaven above' literally. He probably simply stopped appearing to his disciples.

Key Points

1 Mark's Gospel ends with the resurrection of Jesus. The story of his resurrection appearances and the Commission to preach the Gospel given to his disciples were added by an unknown author later.
2 The so-called 'longer ending' includes a reference to three resurrection appearances of Jesus – to Mary Magdalene, to two travellers and to the eleven disciples.
3 The Commission to the disciples includes the 'supernatural' powers that they were to be given. At least two of these are extremely unlikely.
4 The Gospel ends with the ascension of Jesus into heaven. Many Christians feel uncertain about what happened to Jesus at the end of his life.

Work to do

1 a How many different endings to Mark's Gospel are there?
  b Which of the endings appears to be the most likely? Give one reason for your answer.
2 a What is the so-called 'longer ending' to Mark's Gospel?
  b Give one possible reason for the so-called 'longer ending' being attached to Mark's Gospel.
3 a What is meant by the 'Commission' of Jesus which was given to the disciples?
  b Which references in the Commission are thought unlikely to be authentic?

For your Information

According to Mark the last words of Jesus were to his disciples:

"Go into all the world and preach the good news to all creation. Whoever believes and is baptised will be saved and whoever does not believe will be condemned."
(16.15–16)

Many Christians feel unhappy about the picture of Jesus ascending into heaven which is found in Mark and the other Synoptic Gospels.

3.8 Christian belief and the resurrection

Key Question

How important was the resurrection of Jesus to the early Christians?

The fact that Jesus was crucified and brought back to life by God has been at the heart of the Christian faith for two thousand years. The earliest documents in the New Testament are not the Gospels but the letters (epistles) of Paul. Scholars believe that these letters take us back to the earliest form of Christianity since they were written within a few decades of the death of Jesus. They were sent to some of the churches that Paul himself had founded and some of the Christians he had helped.

Paul and the resurrection of Jesus

One of the most important passages in the letters of Paul comes in I Corinthians 15.3–4, where he speaks of the 'Gospel' that he preached when he was in Corinth. This Gospel, Paul insists, was based on three facts:

- the death of Jesus on the cross 'for our sins, according to the Scriptures';
- the burial of Jesus in the tomb, so showing that his death had really taken place;
- the resurrection of Jesus 'on the third day according to the Scriptures'.

As important as the death and burial of Jesus were, though, it was his resurrection from the dead that really excited Paul. He insisted that the resurrection was not a figment of the imagination – it was based on well-substantiated historical evidence. After he rose from the dead Jesus appeared to Peter; the Twelve (the disciples); more than 500 followers at the same time; James, his brother; and the Twelve for a second time. Then, Paul insists, the risen Christ appeared to him – an event that took place when he was dramatically converted to Christianity on the Damascus Road.

Paul makes it clear that the whole Christian message depends on this one belief – that Jesus has been brought back from the dead (see information box). He also goes on to draw out another implication of accepting that Jesus has been raised from the dead – if Jesus has not been brought back to life then there is no such thing as life after death for anyone.

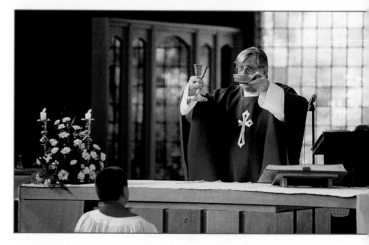

The Eucharist is one of the most important ways that Christians experience the living Christ today.

A question about the resurrection

Towards the end of his ministry Jesus was asked a question about life after death by the Sadducees (12.18–27). Ironically, this group of Jewish believers did not believe in life after death. Jesus made it clear to them that in the next life such normal things as marrying and raising a family would not happen. In that new life believers will be like the angels in heaven – praising God.

Christians today and the risen Jesus

Christians today believe that Jesus is alive. They recognise that, two thousand years after the event, they can never know the details of what happened. The details do not particularly concern them. What matters is that they find Jesus alive with them in the world today. They believe that the living Jesus can be experienced today in two main ways:

1 Through prayer. They pray to God through the living power of Jesus, their Saviour. Prayer is a conversation between Jesus and the believer.

2 Through worship. For most Christians the Eucharist is the most important act of worship. It is in this act of worship that they meet the living Christ as they eat the bread and drink the wine at the altar.

For your Information

Paul wrote to the Christians in Corinth:

"If Christ had not been raised [from the dead], our preaching is useless and so is our faith."

I Corinthians 15.14

Key Points

1 The earliest documents in the New Testament – the letters of Paul – show the importance of the resurrection of Jesus to the Christian faith.
2 Paul produced a list of people to whom Jesus had appeared after he had been brought back to life. The risen Jesus also appeared to him on the Damascus Road.
3 Paul states that if Jesus had not been brought back to life then there cannot be any such thing as life after death.
4 Christians today experience the risen Christ in prayer and worship, especially through celebrating the Eucharist.

Work to do

1 a Which are the earliest documents in the New Testament?
  b Why do scholars think that this is particularly important?
2 a On which three 'facts' did Paul believe the whole Christian message (Gospel) to be based?
  b Which of these three facts did Paul believe to be most important?
  c Why?

In the Glossary

Eucharist • Gospel • New Testament • Paul • Peter

A cross which does not hold a figure of the dying Christ is a symbolic reminder that Jesus rose from the dead.

3.9 Christians and life after death

Key Question

What do Christians believe about life after death?

Jesus spoke from time to time about life after death and made it clear that he was offering his listeners an unending life beyond the grave – a spiritual life which they would share with him and God the Father in the Kingdom of God (heaven).

Eternal life

Jesus taught that eternal life was so valuable that any sensible person would make any sacrifice to possess it. He even suggested on one occasion that a person should be prepared to pluck out their eye or cut off their leg if either was causing them to lose their faith in God (9.43, 45). Jesus used this very strong, symbolic example like a parable to make an important point.

To underline the same important message Jesus told Peter and the other disciples that anyone who leaves behind the things that are most precious to them for God's sake will receive spiritual rewards in this life and eternal life 'in the age to come' (10.28–31). Two other disciples, James and John, came to Jesus on another occasion and asked that they might be given the most important seats in heaven (10.35–45). It was a request that Jesus took seriously, but he told his two

disciples that the reward they were looking for was not his to give – this power was God's alone. For Jesus eternal life meant sharing God's glory.

At the last meal that Jesus shared with his disciples he gave them some bread to eat and some wine to drink. When he handed them the wine goblet everyone drank from it. Jesus told them:

> "This is my blood which is poured out for many, my blood which seals God's covenant. I tell you, I will never again drink this wine until the day I will drink the new wine in the kingdom of God." 14.25

It was heaven that Jesus was looking forward to here. For him it lay beyond his death and resurrection. It would follow the time when he was reunited with his Father, God, and would be shared with all those who had responded to his call to be one of his disciples. There is no indication in Mark, or in any of the Gospels, of what eternal life would be like, but only that it would be spent in the presence of God the Father and Jesus. This was all his disciples needed to know.

This gravestone expresses a strong Christian belief in life after death. When confronted with death Christians find this belief very comforting.

The Christian belief in life after death

Their belief in life after death offers Christians today:

1 A way of understanding the suffering of this life. For many people this life must seem to be very unfair. Some people suffer a great deal, while others barely suffer at all. This thought is often in the minds of those who suffer. They find the answer in looking forward to a time when all injustices would be righted – in heaven.

2 A way of understanding the sadness of death. All Christian funeral services underline that death is not the end and that heaven awaits. Here everyone will be reunited with loved ones who have 'gone on before'.

3 A way of facing up to the divine judgement which comes for everyone at the end of life. In the past it has been taught that people will be sent to heaven or hell as a result of this judgement. Although many Christians no longer believe in the existence of a literal heaven and hell, their belief in life after death does have a substantial effect on the way that they live their lives here and now.

Key Points

1 Jesus left his followers with a strong belief in life after death. He spoke about it on may occasions.
2 Jesus told his disciples that eternal life is more precious than any earthly possession.
3 Life after death puts the suffering of this life into perspective, helps people to understand death and reminds people of God's coming judgement.

Work to do

1 a What did Jesus mean when he spoke of 'eternal life'?
  b What did Jesus have to say about eternal life?
2 a Which two disciples asked Jesus if they have the best seats in heaven reserved for them?
  b What reply did Jesus give to them and what did he mean by it?

Having shared some bread and wine with his disciples, Jesus looked forward to the day in heaven when they would all share a banquet together.

In the Glossary

Gospel • Kingdom of God • Peter

Read

Mark
1.14–15;
4.26–34;
10.13–16

 **Key Question**

What did Jesus teach about the Kingdom of God, and how did he do it?

After John the Baptist had been thrown into prison (he would soon be executed), Jesus returned to Galilee, far from the scene of his baptism and temptation. His purpose was to proclaim the 'Good News' (the Gospel). The first recorded words of Jesus in Mark's Gospel sum up his message:

> "The right time has come … and the Kingdom of God is near! Turn away from [repent] your sins and believe the Good News!"
> (1.15)

Jesus came to call people to change direction in their lives: that is what the word 'repent' means. They were to have faith in the Good News (the Gospel) which announced that God's kingdom had arrived with Jesus. He had come to bring the Gospel – and God's kingdom. This kingdom was shown first in the life of Jesus, and then in the lives of his followers.

The mystery of God's kingdom

One of the things that Mark is anxious to explain is that the coming of God's kingdom is silent, unnoticed by many people. This fact, and the way that God chose to introduce God's rule (kingdom) through a Messiah who suffered, are two points that Mark emphasises throughout his Gospel. This is the 'mystery of the kingdom' which is the subject of many of the parables that Jesus told.

Jesus explained to the people how they could enter this kingdom. On one occasion parents brought their children to Jesus, but the disciples turned them away. This made Jesus very angry and he said:

> "Let the children come to me, and do not stop them, because the Kingdom of God belongs to such as these. I assure you that whoever does not receive the Kingdom of God like a child will never enter it."
> (10.14–15)

Just as a child relies on adults to look after it, so anyone entering the kingdom must depend totally on (show faith in) God.

Jesus did not say that God's kingdom had begun – only that it was near. Throughout Mark's Gospel Jesus was reluctant to give many specific details about the kingdom. Towards the end of his life Jesus explained the reason for his reluctance:

> "No one knows … when that hour or day will come – neither the angels in heaven, nor the Son; only the Father knows."
> (13.32)

Instead, Jesus encouraged people to imagine what God's kingdom was like. He did this by using many stories (parables) to teach them.

Good teachers make their teaching relevant to how people live their lives.

Parables and God's kingdom

For his parables about the Kingdom of God Jesus often turned to nature. Here is one example (4.26–29). Jesus, and those who follow him, are just like a man who scatters seed in a field. While the man works hard by day, and sleeps by night, the seed is busy growing in the earth. The man does not understand just how this happens, but he doesn't need to know. It is the soil itself which provides the necessary nutrients that each seed needs to grow into healthy corn – the tender stalk, the ear and the full weight

The parable of the seed growing in the ground inspires those who have the task of preaching about the Kingdom of God.

of the corn. It is only when the harvest is ripe that the man gathers in the corn. In a similar way, the Kingdom of God grows until the end of time when God gathers in the harvest.

Rather than give concrete information about God's kingdom, then, Jesus left his listeners with a series of stories about it. Mark tells us that Jesus 'told them as much as they could understand' (4.33), and that he only did this in parables. When he was alone with his disciples, however, 'he would explain everything to them' (4.34). The problem was that they did not understand what he was talking about.

Key Points

1 Preaching about the Kingdom of God was the most important activity in the ministry of Jesus. He mainly did this by using parables.
2 The mystery of God's kingdom was that it had come through the ministry of Jesus – and yet was still to come fully in the future.
3 Jesus often turned to nature for his parables about the Kingdom of God. Rather than provide information the parables were designed to raise questions in the minds of his listeners. They were puzzles that needed to be solved.

For your Information

There are many parables in Mark about the Kingdom of God. Amongst them are:
a The lamp under a bowl (4.21–22)
b New cloth on an old coat (2.21)
c New wine in old wineskins (2.22)
d The sower and the soils (4.3–8, 14–20)
e The mustard seed (4.30–32)
f The growing seed (4.26–29)

In the Glossary

Gospel • Kingdom of God • Mark • Parable

Work to do

1 What did Jesus mean when he spoke about the 'Kingdom of God'?
2 What did Jesus say about the coming of God's kingdom?
3 What did Jesus encourage people to do by only speaking to them in parables about the coming of God's kingdom?
4 Describe one parable in which Jesus spoke about God's kingdom. Why do you think that he used this particular picture, and what might he have wanted his listeners to learn from it?

4.2 The sower

Read

Mark
4.1–20

Key Question

What was Jesus saying about the Kingdom of God in his parable of the sower?

Jesus took refuge from the crowds on board a boat, anchored just off shore. From there he delivered the first parable in Mark's Gospel, which is told at length and explained in detail. The parable of the sower, one of the most well-known stories that Jesus told, used the familiar sight in Palestine of a farmer scattering his seed to the left and right as he walked up and down his field. There may even have been a Galilean farmer actually sowing his seed on the hillside above at the time – if so, it would have made the parable even more vivid.

The parable of the sower

This story is very unusual as it is followed, almost directly, by an interpretation. That does not happen with any other parable in Mark's Gospel, or indeed in the other Gospels. From this interpretation, which probably came from the early Church and not Jesus, the progress of God's kingdom amongst different groups of people can be understood. In Palestine the sowing of the seed came before the ploughing of the ground and so some parts of the field did not offer suitable conditions for the seed to thrive:

- some fell on the pathway, allowing the birds to gobble it up (4.3);
- some fell on ground where limestone lay just beneath the surface and so the earth was very shallow. The seed could not take root and the sun scorched it quickly (4.5);
- some fell among thorn bushes (4.7) which choked the young seed.

Farmers in Palestine knew that they would lose much of their seed each year, and there was little they could do about it. They knew that some parts of their land were better than others, but they had to use all the space they had. They were satisfied as long as some of the seed fell into good ground – sprouting, growing, producing a good yield. Even the plants that did grow, however, produced a variable yield – some thirty-fold, some sixty-fold and some a hundred-fold. This is one of the main points that the parable makes.

Understanding the parable

Mark turns the parable into an allegory in which each point in the story carries its own meaning. The sower, Jesus, and those who follow after him as his disciples, sow God's message. Those who receive it fall into different groups:

- Some are like the seeds that fall by the wayside (4.15). The ground of their heart is so hard that the seed does not penetrate the surface. They are so 'hardened' to the message about God's kingdom that as soon as they hear it Satan, the Evil One, snatches it away from them and it is lost.
- Some people are like the seeds that fall on rocky ground (4.16). When they hear the message they are pleased, but it does not really sink in. They let go of it as soon as persecution or trouble comes along.

Entering the Kingdom of God is a challenge to people – they must struggle to find their way into it.

- Some people are like the seeds that fall among the thorn bushes (4.18). As soon as they hear the message the cares of this world, or the love of money, choke and kill it.
- Some people are like the seed that falls into the fertile ground – and grows. They become committed followers of Jesus. Even then, though, some people are more fruitful and productive in their work for God than others.

The purpose of parables

When Jesus was alone, some of those who heard his parables came with his twelve disciples seeking an explanation. Why, they wondered, did Jesus speak to them in parables? The answer that Jesus gave them was very mysterious, and not what Mark's readers would have expected. It fell into two parts:

1 To his disciples, the secret of God's kingdom has been given. They do not need Jesus to speak to them in parables.

2 Others, 'who are on the outside', can only receive the truth through stories. Why? Because stories make the truth simpler? No! Parables actually make it more difficult to understand!

> "They may look and look, yet not see; they may listen and listen, yet not understand. For if they did, they would turn to God, and he would forgive them."
> (4.12)

Key Points

1 The parable of the sower is unusual – it has the interpretation attached. Usually the listeners were left to work out the interpretation for themselves.
2 The parable of the different kinds of soil into which the seed is sown, is about the different reception which people gave to the teaching of Jesus.
3 The parable ends with a comment on the purpose of parables. The disciples did not need to be taught in parables. They already knew the secret of God's kingdom. The parables actually made it harder for others to understand the message of Jesus – a somewhat strange thing for Jesus to have said!

A church is decorated for its annual harvest festival. This theme provides an obvious link with the parable of the sower.

Work to do

1 a What makes this parable unique amongst all those told by Jesus?
 b In this parable, how many different kinds of soil are mentioned and what are they?
 c How did Jesus use the different kinds of soil to explain the different ways that people receive the message about God's kingdom?
2 Look at the words of Jesus attached to the parable in Mark 4.12 (left).
 a Try to explain what you think these words might possibly mean.
 b Why do you think these words seem to be very strange if they actually came from Jesus?
3 Describe in detail the parable of the sower. Explain why it is often called an allegory.

In the Glossary

Allegory • Disciple • Kingdom of God • Parable • Satan

4.3 The rich man

 Read

Mark 10.17–31

 **Key Question**

What do we learn from the encounter with the rich man about Jesus' attitude towards wealth?

Nowhere is the cost of entering God's kingdom brought out more clearly than in the story of the rich man who had absolutely everything – except eternal life. He wanted eternal life desperately but was unwilling to give up his wealth to obtain it. There is, however, no other way to enter the kingdom, and this was a lesson that even Peter and the other disciples had to learn as well (10.28).

Money – and its dangers

The unnamed stranger approached Jesus with the direct question:

> "Good Teacher, what must I do to receive eternal life?"
> (10.17)

In answering his question, Jesus reminded the stranger of the Ten Commandments which were the foundation on which every Jew built his or her life. Jesus chose to remind him of those commandments that emphasised his responsibilities to his fellow human beings rather than his duty towards God. The man replied that he had kept these commandments since he was a child, and Jesus did not contradict him. Jesus recognised the man's sincerity and goodness. He was certainly not a hypocrite.

Just occasionally in Mark's Gospel an individual is seen as someone special. Mark tells us that Jesus loved the man standing in front of him. The only thing lacking was that he was not yet a disciple. One thing stood in the way of this:

> "Go and sell all you have and give the money to the poor, and you will have riches in heaven; and come and follow me."
> (10.21)

Mark describes graphically the effect that the words of Jesus had on the man – gloom spread over his face and he went away sad. He couldn't bear to give away all his riches.

The incident then turned into a lesson for his disciples. Jesus provoked them with the words:

> "How hard it will be for rich people to enter the Kingdom of God!"
> (10.23)

The opening letters of each of the Ten Commandments, written in Hebrew, are found on the wall of every synagogue. They are a reminder of the importance of these laws to every Jew – as they were to the rich man who met Jesus.

As Jews, the disciples found this very difficult to understand. The teaching of the Jewish Scriptures was that wealth was a sign of God's blessing – not the opposite. If this man could not be saved, and be brought into eternal life, then who could? Jesus replied that the very things that seem impossible to human eyes are more than possible with God.

Leaving everything

Jesus is not saying that anyone who wants to be a disciple must give up all of their earthly possessions, although for some it may involve that. There are many examples of men and women, in the past and present, who have left home, family and friends to serve God elsewhere. Jesus, though, is saying something slightly different here. The demands that Jesus makes vary from person to person. For Peter, Andrew, James and John it meant leaving their occupation and family behind. For Matthew it involved leaving the employment of the Romans and returning all the money that he had taken illegally.

Yet, as Jesus went on to point out, those who are wealthy do have a particular problem when they are confronted by the demands of discipleship. He said to his disciples:

> "It is much harder for a rich person to enter the Kingdom of God than for a camel to go through the eye of a needle." (10.25)

No one is absolutely sure what Jesus meant by this. He probably had in mind a very low gate into Jerusalem which was called the Needle's Eye. It was extremely low to prevent enemy soldiers from infiltrating the city in large numbers while it was dark. A camel had a real struggle to enter the city by this gate but, as night fell, it was the only way to get into Jerusalem.

The meaning for today

This incident carries implications for those who would become disciples of Jesus today. Just as in the time of Jesus, money and riches very often distort the way a person looks at life. In spending a lifetime increasing his or her wealth, a person may neglect the much more important spiritual side of life. Commitment to God may well involve the changing of priorities. Much of a person's money may need to be redirected into new and more useful channels. For some people that is a very high, or impossible, price to pay.

Key Points

1 The rich man who came to Jesus wanted to enter God's kingdom. When challenged by Jesus he stated that he had kept all of the Ten Commandments from his earliest days – a claim that Jesus didn't challenge.
2 Jesus told him that he must sell everything to enter God's kingdom. His riches were the main barrier standing in his way.
3 The demands made on those who would enter God's kingdom vary from person to person. Anything that stands in the way, though, must be removed first.

Work to do

1 Jesus said:

"This is impossible for man, but not for God; everything is possible for God." (10.27)

  a To which group of people did Jesus speak these words?
  b Why did Jesus say them?
  c What was Jesus trying to teach by saying these words?
2 Peter told Jesus that his disciples had left everything to follow him. What did Jesus say his disciples would receive in return?
3 What do you think that Jesus meant when he spoke of 'riches in heaven'?

In the Glossary

Andrew • Disciple • Gospel • James • John • Kingdom of God • Matthew • Peter • Ten Commandments

4.4 Divorce

Read

Mark
10.1–12

**Key
Question**

**What did
Jesus teach
about
divorce?**

We have just seen the cost of the Kingdom of God (Unit 4.3). In this unit we see what Jesus had to say about the area in life in which the closest of human relations are to be found – marriage. Jesus made it clear that in God's kingdom the lifelong dedication of one person to another in marriage is demanded. This is so costly that the disciples, in Matthew's account of the words of Jesus (19.1–15), said that it would be better to avoid marrying altogether.

In Mark's Gospel, marriage is seen within the context of the Kingdom of God. Marriage is not just a human arrangement but is how God has arranged and planned for human happiness in his kingdom. Divorce, then, can only be a denial of God's plan and purpose.

A controversial issue

As Jesus entered Judea he was moving even closer to Jerusalem – and death. The tension mounted as the crowds came flocking to hear him teaching beside the River Jordan. Some Pharisees approached Jesus and tried to trap him by asking a question about divorce. This was a very controversial issue within the Jewish community.

The Jewish Scriptures laid down that a man could divorce his wife if she was guilty of some form of behaviour that he did not like (Deuteronomy 24.1). The problem was caused by the vagueness of deciding what behaviour fell into this category. This led to the growth of two clear schools of Jewish thought at the time of Jesus:

a The teaching of Rabbi Hillel. He taught that a man could divorce his wife for the most trivial of reasons, for example if she did not keep the house properly, or if she was in the habit of burning his dinner.

b The teaching of Rabbi Shammai. He taught his followers that the teaching of the Scriptures referred to adultery alone, and this was the only acceptable ground for divorce.

The teaching of Jesus

Jesus confronted his questioners with the teaching that lay behind the ruling of Moses in the Old Testament book of Deuteronomy. Moses had only allowed divorce there because the Jews were so hard to teach. The Jews refused to allow the hard demands of God to rule their lives, and Jesus saw this as a barrier to people who wanted to enter God's kingdom. In God's kingdom new rules would apply. It meant returning to the original plans that God had for the human race:

"in the beginning, at the time of creation, God made them male and female."
(10.6)

According to the earliest Jewish Scriptures, the purpose of marriage is for a man and a woman to be lifelong companions. This relationship cannot be broken:

"for this reason a man will leave his father and mother and unite with his wife, and the two will become one. So they are no longer two, but one. Man must not separate, then, what God has joined together."
(10.7–9)

When Jesus was alone with his disciples he explained his teaching to them. A man who divorces his wife and marries another, commits adultery with his second wife. Jesus added that the same applied to a woman who divorced and remarried. This, though, was something that could not happen, since women had no rights of divorce in the Jewish community.

The teaching of Jesus today

There is some disagreement today amongst the different Christian Churches about divorce. They all agree, however, about the desirability of marriage being a permanent, lifelong agreement between a man and a woman. That is fully in keeping with the teaching of Jesus. In many Churches attempts are made to support this teaching by providing help and advice for those approaching marriage and those experiencing problems in their married lives. In most Churches, however, it is recognised that many marriages (over one in three, and increasing all the time) end in divorce.

Many Christians today are as worried about remarriage as about divorce. In most Free Churches people can remarry through a full church wedding service. A few Anglican churches offer this, but most provide only a church blessing after the couple have first married in a registry office. To Roman Catholics, however, marriage is a sacrament which cannot be broken. Even if a Roman Catholic couple go through a civil divorce, they remain married in the eyes of the Church. They can, however, apply for an 'annulment' in certain circumstances, which is a declaration that the marriage never took place.

For your Information

Jesus referred to divorce several times in his teaching. You can find references elsewhere in:
a Matthew 19.1–12;
b Luke 16.18;
c Matthew 5.31–32.

Key Points

1 In God's kingdom the dedication of one person to another in marriage is demanded.
2 There were two schools of thought about divorce in the Jewish community in the time of Jesus – one strict and the other very lax.
3 When questioned about divorce Jesus spoke about the original plan of God for marriage – one man to one woman for life.
4 Christians today disagree about divorce.

In the Glossary

Anglican Church • Disciple • Free Churches • Jerusalem • Kingdom of God • Moses • Pharisees • Roman Catholic Church • Sacrament

Work to do

1 a What does Jesus say about marriage and divorce in Mark's Gospel?
  b How did the teaching of Jesus on divorce differ from that of the rabbis?
  c How far do you think that Jesus' teaching about divorce in Mark's Gospel is practical in the modern world?
2 a What was the Jewish teaching about divorce in the time of Jesus?
  b What did Jesus say about the laws that Moses gave to the Jewish people?
3 Why do you think that Jesus took his listeners back to God's original intention for marriage when giving his own teaching?

Although divorce was allowed at the time of Jesus, the importance that Jews attached to marriage was considerable.

4.5 The greatest commandments

 Read

Mark
12.28–34;
12.41–44

 **Key Question**

Which commandment did Jesus say was the most important – and why?

A rabbi reads from a scroll of the Torah in a synagogue. This service is taking place in a Reformed synagogue, as women are not allowed to play a public role in Orthodox Jewish services.

Scribes were important members of the Jewish community who, as lawyers, interpreted the Law of Moses (the Torah) and answered the many queries of the people about its application to their everyday lives. In the laws that Moses had passed on to the Jewish people from God there were 613 commandments (mitzvot) altogether – some negative ('Thou shalt not . . .') and some positive ('Thou shalt . . .'). The Ten Commandments lay at the heart of the Torah. In theory, each of these commandments carried equal value for each Jew, but the scribe who came to Jesus with his question wanted to know whether, in practice, one was more important than the others. Orthodox Jews today still try to keep as many of the original laws as possible.

How Jesus answered the scribe

The way that Jesus treated the scribe suggests that he was questioning Jesus in a genuine and sincere manner. He was not trying to trick Jesus as others had done. The reply that Jesus gave him contained nothing new – it was drawn from the Jewish Scriptures, which would have been very familiar to the scribe. In his answer, as we shall see, Jesus placed love for God at the heart of the Law; love for one's neighbour could, and should, spring from a person's love for God.

שְׁמַע יִשְׂרָאֵל, יהוה אֱלֹהֵינוּ, יהוה אֶחָד.*¹

—In an undertone— בָּרוּךְ שֵׁם כְּבוֹד מַלְכוּתוֹ לְעוֹלָם וָעֶד.

Some congregations complete the first chapter of *Shema* (following paragraph) at this point, although most omit it. However if you fear that you will not recite the full *Shema* later in *Shacharis* before the prescribed time has elapsed, recite all three chapters of *Shema* (p. 90) here.

דברים ו:ח-ט

וְאָהַבְתָּ אֵת יהוה אֱלֹהֶיךָ, בְּכָל לְבָבְךָ, וּבְכָל נַפְשְׁךָ, וּבְכָל מְאֹדֶךָ. וְהָיוּ הַדְּבָרִים הָאֵלֶּה, אֲשֶׁר אָנֹכִי מְצַוְּךָ הַיּוֹם, עַל לְבָבֶךָ. וְשִׁנַּנְתָּם לְבָנֶיךָ, וְדִבַּרְתָּ בָּם, בְּשִׁבְתְּךָ בְּבֵיתֶךָ, וּבְלֶכְתְּךָ בַדֶּרֶךְ, וּבְשָׁכְבְּךָ וּבְקוּמֶךָ. וּקְשַׁרְתָּם לְאוֹת עַל יָדֶךָ, וְהָיוּ לְטֹטָפֹת בֵּין עֵינֶיךָ. וּכְתַבְתָּם עַל מְזֻזוֹת בֵּיתֶךָ וּבִשְׁעָרֶיךָ.

אַתָּה הוּא* עַד שֶׁלֹּא נִבְרָא הָעוֹלָם, אַתָּה הוּא מִשֶּׁנִּבְרָא הָעוֹלָם, אַתָּה הוּא בָּעוֹלָם הַזֶּה, וְאַתָּה הוּא לָעוֹלָם הַבָּא. ✧ קַדֵּשׁ אֶת שִׁמְךָ עַל מַקְדִּישֵׁי שְׁמֶךָ,* וְקַדֵּשׁ אֶת שִׁמְךָ בְּעוֹלָמֶךָ. וּבִישׁוּעָתְךָ תָּרִים וְתַגְבִּיהַּ קַרְנֵנוּ. בָּרוּךְ אַתָּה יהוה, מְקַדֵּשׁ אֶת שִׁמְךָ בָּרַבִּים.* (אָמֵן.—Cong.)

The Shema on display in a synagogue. The Shema goes to the very heart of the Jewish faith.

Jesus summarised the teaching of the Law by referring to the most important Jewish statement of faith – the Shema. The Shema is the Hebrew word for 'hear', which is the first word of Deuteronomy 6.4. The Shema goes on to say:

> "Listen, Israel! The Lord our God is the only Lord. Love the Lord your God with all your heart, with all your soul, with all your mind, and with all your strength." (12.29–30)

The Shema goes to the very heart of the Jewish religion. It expresses the central belief that there is only one God, and that all Jews must love him with their whole being. It is still repeated regularly in religious worship since it expresses the aspirations of every Jewish man and woman. Jesus went on to provide his understanding of the second most important commandment by quoting from Leviticus 19.18:

> "Love your neighbour as you love yourself." (12.31)

To Jewish people, familiar with this quotation from their Scriptures, the word 'neighbour' would have applied to any fellow countryman or fellow believer. In the words of Jesus, however, the meaning was extended to cover any person, of any race. This change of emphasis formed the basis of the most well known of all the parables of Jesus, that of the Good Samaritan, in Luke 10.25–37.

Key Points

1 The Law was at the heart of Jewish religion. The Ten Commandments were at the centre of the Law.
2 A scribe wanted to know the greatest of the commandments. Jesus answered the question by referring to the Shema – the Jewish statement of faith. It says there is one God only and all Jews must love him with their whole being. They must love their neighbour as much as themselves.

Work to do

1 a Which two commandments did Jesus say were the most important?
  b Where did these two commandments come from?
  c How important are these commandments for Christians today?
2 a 'Which commandment is the most important of all?' Who did this question come from and how did Jesus react to it?
  b How did the scribe react to the answer that Jesus gave?

In the Glossary

Moses • Parable • Scribe • Shema • Ten Commandments • Torah

Read

Mark
5.21–34

Key Question

How important was faith in the work of Jesus?

Faith in the Gospels covers a wide area of human trust and trustworthiness. It merges into love at one end of the scale and into loyalty and devotion at the other. Both love and loyalty are important aspects of faith – especially faith in God. Within Judaism and Christianity faith also includes 'belief' – accepting certain things as true about God and what he has done in the world. Christians, for example, believe (have faith in) the resurrection of Jesus from the dead. This means that they accept it as true and live their lives in the light of it. For them Jesus is alive today. In the teaching of Jesus 'faith' involved seeing that God was working through him, building up the Kingdom of God on earth.

Two miracles

This unit brings together prayer and faith. We will look at two miracles – the raising of Jairus' daughter from the dead (5.21–24, 35–43; see Unit 5.3) and the healing of the woman with a haemorrhage (5.25–34; see Unit 5.4) – which were brought together by Mark, and interwoven into one story, because they had a common theme. This theme is the importance of showing faith – trust – in Jesus, even when the situation appears to be hopeless. They also have secondary themes which link them to each other – the person who receives the healing touch of Jesus in each case is female, and the person in need is beyond the help of normal medicine. A divine miracle is the only hope – and that is where faith really comes into its own.

These two accounts contain many important details.

1 Jairus, a Gentile, showed his faith in Jesus to help his daughter even though others around him said that he was wasting his own time and that of Jesus. Mark draws our attention to the man's faith when he tells us that he came to Jesus and pleaded 'earnestly' with him. This was a man who was desperate for divine help. Even when he returned home with Jesus and found that his daughter had died in the meantime he still believed that some kind of miracle was possible. True faith is the opposite of doubt.

Believing in the resurrection of Jesus gives Christians a depth to their lives which they could not receive in any other way.

2 In a similar way the woman who touched the hem of the garment of Jesus was just as desperate for his help. She had suffered from a blood haemorrhage for twelve years and had spent all of her savings in seeking medical help. No one had been able to help her. She pushed her way through the crowd to reach Jesus and simply touched his cloak as he walked past. This was a simple act of faith on her part since there is no other indication in the Gospels of someone touching Jesus and being healed.

The woman hoped to be swallowed up in the anonymity of the crowd. Jesus, though, knew that something special had happened and he tried to discover the woman's identity. To Mark this was a very important part of his story. It took great faith, and courage, from the woman to confess her situation to Jesus in front of the listening crowd. It also added an important dimension to her healing. Jesus told her to 'Go in peace'. Her body was healed but she was spiritually healed and forgiven as well. It was her faith in Jesus which had brought her spiritual salvation. She was now a member of God's kingdom. Her simple act of faith had a much greater implication than she ever realised.

Key Points

1 Faith in the Gospels included love, loyalty and belief.
2 Jairus had faith that Jesus could even bring his daughter back to life from the dead.
3 The woman with the haemorrhage believed that she would be cured even if she only touched the cloak of Jesus.
4 Jesus told the woman that spiritual salvation as well as physical healing had been given to her.

Work to do

1 Write three sentences to show that you understand the meaning of the word 'faith' as it is used in the Gospels.
2 a Read Mark 8.11–13. Why do you think that Jesus 'sighed deeply' when the Pharisees made their request of Jesus?
  b Explain why, in the light of the miracles of Jairus' daughter and the woman with the haemorrhage, you believe that Jesus turned down the request of the Pharisees.
3 The woman with a haemorrhage was an outcast in Jewish society for two reasons – she was a woman and her constant flow of blood made her religiously 'unclean'. Is there a message in this miracle for people who are treated like outcasts in society today? If so, what do you think that message is?

In the Glossary

Gospel • Kingdom of God • New Testament • Synagogue

Worshipping provides Christians with the opportunity to express their faith and devotion to God.

5.2 Prayer

Read

Mark
6.45–46

Key Question

What do we learn about prayer in Mark's Gospel?

Throughout his ministry Jesus was concerned to develop his relationship with God, his Father. Mark records many occasions when Jesus prayed to God – especially when he had an important decision to make, when the people were making heavy demands on him or when he faced a severe challenge.

Jesus and prayer in Mark's Gospel

Mark describes three occasions on which Jesus prayed:

1 1.32–38. This refers to an early incident in the life of Jesus. Jesus had driven an evil spirit out of a man in the synagogue in Capernaum. Mark tells us that the people in the town were amazed at the authority which Jesus showed. That night, after sunset, they brought all the sick and demon-possessed out into the streets so that Jesus could heal them. Mark gives us a graphic description of the scene: 'The whole town gathered at the door.' Early next morning, we are told, Jesus got up while it was dark and took himself off to a 'solitary place' where he prayed. Jesus was obviously using this time spent with God to recharge his batteries before facing the next demand on his spiritual and physical resources.

2 6.30–46. As he was feeding a large crowd of people from the slender resources of five loaves and two fishes, Jesus gave God thanks for the food. It was the Jewish custom to thank God for everything – including food. As soon as the miracle was completed, and the scraps of food were cleared up, Jesus sent his disciples away to the other side of the lake. Then, after dismissing the crowd, he went up a mountainside to pray. He did this although there would have been many people in the crowd who wanted his help. Prayer took precedence over everything else for Jesus.

3 14.35–36. After sharing his last meal with his disciples and, with the shadow of the cross growing closer and closer, Jesus took Peter, James and John with him into the Garden of Gethsemane. Here we find Jesus

Christians believe that personal prayer is sometimes necessary if one is to live the Christian life as God intended.

at his most troubled and desperate. He knows that only loneliness and suffering lie ahead. He hopes that, even now, they can be avoided but he comes to understand, and accept, where the will of God is leading him.

For Jesus prayer was not the last resort – it was the first. So it is for many Christians. This is why prayer plays such an important part in all acts of Christian worship. Christians pray for themselves and their own needs but they also pray for others.

Prayer and faith

In the life of Jesus there was a close link between prayer and faith. He had a deep faith that God would hear, and answer, his prayers. He encouraged his disciples to have the same faith in God. Mark gives us the

Christians often feel comforted and strengthened when they know that other people are praying for them.

example of the disciples struggling, unsuccessfully, to heal an epileptic boy (9.14–29). They couldn't do so. After Jesus had healed the boy the disciples wanted to know why they had failed. Jesus told them: 'This kind [of evil spirit] can come out only by prayer.' Jesus was teaching them an important lesson – miracles can only be achieved if the prayer to God for help is accompanied by real faith. It is the faith that matters – not the prayer.

Key Points

1 Jesus believed in prayer.
2 Jesus used the solitude of praying to recover from the demands that other people made on him.
3 Jesus followed the Jewish custom of thanking God for the provision of his daily food.
4 Jesus prayed for himself in the Garden of Gethsemane that he might have the strength to accept the will of God.

Work to do

1 Describe an instance when Jesus prayed:
   a when the demands the people were making on him were too great;
   b to give thanks for food that God had miraculously provided;
   c when he felt alone and deserted.
2 What is the link between prayer and faith in Mark's Gospel?

In the Glossary

Disciple • Gospel • Mark • Peter • Synagogue

5.3 Jairus' daughter

Read

Mark
5.21–24;
5.35–43

Key Question

What is unusual about Mark's account of Jesus healing the daughter of Jairus?

This story concerns an area where the power of God's kingdom had not yet been shown by Jesus – over death. The healing of the daughter of Jairus (see photograph) shows Jesus as the Lord of both life and death. Typically, though, Mark sandwiches it around another story of healing – that of a very needy woman. These two miracles had much in common in Mark's mind. They both concern females, one young and the other older, who had passed beyond all normal medical help. The link between them is that of faith, since both Jairus and the woman with a haemorrhage (see Unit 5.4) showed great faith in Jesus.

The miracle described

For this miracle Jesus returned to the western side of the Lake of Galilee where he was greeted by a large crowd. Jairus, 'an official of the local synagogue', arrived and threw himself at the feet of Jesus. Jairus knew that his daughter was dying but believed that, even now, a touch from Jesus would restore her to health. As Jairus was an important man in the Jewish community many people would have been surprised at his action. He explained his desperate need to Jesus:

> "My little daughter is very ill. Please come and place your hands on her, so that she will get well and live!"
> (5.23)

Like most of the miracles in Mark's Gospel, this one follows a clearly defined pattern: first, the condition of the person is spelled out, then the method of healing is described.

The ruler's daughter is at the point of dying. After an interruption by someone else, also seeking a cure, the man is desperate for help, but while he is with Jesus he is told by messengers that his daughter has died. They add the piece of advice:

> "Why bother the Teacher any longer?"
> (5.35)

'Teacher' is an unusual title for Jesus, which is used only on one other occasion in Mark's Gospel (9.17).

When the news of the girl's death reached Jesus he paid no attention to it but simply said:

> "Don't be afraid, only believe."
> (5.36)

Jesus then took his three closest companions – Simon Peter, James and John – with him to the girl's house to discover that the weeping and wailing, which always accompanied death in a Jewish household, had already begun. The response of Jesus to this, though, is rather unexpected. He told the people that the girl was not really dead but only sleeping. The scorn with which this statement was received by the onlookers was intense. Jesus returned to the girl's room,

There is some doubt in Mark's account whether Jesus actually brought this girl back from the dead. Mark suggests she was only sleeping.

took her by the hand and said to her 'Talitha kaum' which means, in Aramaic, 'Little girl, I tell you to get up.' At once the twelve-year-old got to her feet and began to walk around. Everyone was amazed to see this, but Jesus told them to say nothing about the incident to anyone.

Was it a miracle?

The comment of Jesus that the child was not dead, but only sleeping, makes us wonder whether this was a miracle or not. If the girl was really raised from the dead then this is the only instance of such a miracle, apart from the resurrection of Jesus, in Mark's Gospel (see information box). We do know that the early Church, to which Mark belonged, did develop the habit of referring to death as 'sleeping', and that may well be the case here. You will find the same reference to death as a form of sleeping on many gravestones (see photograph).

For Mark, though, this was not the important issue. What mattered to him was the meaning that the story carried. Once again, faith holds the key to understanding the miracle, although on this occasion it is the faith of the father and not the child that is highlighted. Early Christians would have understood this miracle as pointing forward to the most important event in Christian history – the rising of Jesus from the dead. Both events told Christians that death was not the end of everything and that life, eternal life, lay beyond death. Jesus has power over death – as shown both in this incident and in his own resurrection.

For your Information

There are only three instances of Jesus bringing the dead back to life in the four Gospels:
a The daughter of Jairus (Matthew 9.18–19, 23–25; Mark 5.22–24, 35–43; Luke 8.41–42, 49–56)
b The widow's son at Nain (Luke 7.11–15)
c Lazarus (John 11.1–44).

In the Glossary

Gospel • James • John • Peter • Synagogue

IN TREASURED MEMORY OF
STELLA RICHARDSON
WHO FELL ASLEEP NOV · 4TH 1952
AFTER A PAINFUL ILLNESS
BRAVELY AND PATIENTLY BORNE
AGED 47.
SOME DAY OUR EYES SHALL SEE
THE FACE WE KEEP IN MEMORY,
AND GOD WILL ...

Key Points

1 The bringing back to life of Jairus' daughter is an important miracle in Mark. Jesus only had his three closest friends – Peter, James and John – with him when he performed the miracle.
2 Jesus surprised everyone by saying that the girl was not dead but sleeping. He commanded her to get to her feet.
3 For early Christians this miracle pointed forward to the resurrection of Jesus from the dead.

Work to do

1 When Jesus was confronted by the confusion in the house of Jairus he said to those around:

"Why all this confusion? Why are you crying? The child is not dead – she is only sleeping."
(5.39)

a What is it that makes this 'miracle' almost unique in Mark's Gospel?
b What are two possible ways of understanding these words of Jesus?
c Why do you think that Jesus told the people not to talk about what he had done afterwards?
2 a How is faith an important element in the story of the healing of Jairus' daughter?
b What do you think that Jesus meant when he said to Jairus: 'Don't be afraid, only believe'?

The Christian practice of drawing a parallel between death and sleep might provide a way of understanding this miracle.

5.4 The woman with a haemorrhage

Read

Mark
5.25–34

Key Question

Why did Mark consider the incident of Jesus healing the woman with a haemorrhage to be important?

Just like the healing of the daughter of Jairus (see Unit 5.3), so the incident in which Jesus cured a woman who had a menstrual blood haemorrhage, or a vaginal infection, bears all the usual hallmarks of a miracle story in Mark's Gospel: the woman's medical condition is explained, and the unusual means of healing her is described.

The illness and the healing

The seriousness of the woman's condition is underlined by the length of time she had suffered from it – twelve years. During this time her doctors had failed to improve her ailment, despite her spending all of her money seeking a cure. She seemed to have been suffering from some form of vaginal bleeding which, under Jewish law, made her religiously unclean and so excluded her from taking part in any form of religious worship (Leviticus 15.25–30). The constant bleeding also weakened her physically so that she felt desperately tired.

In the crush of people trying to reach Jesus, the woman thought that she could safely touch him without being noticed. We have no other example of a person being cured in this way, but the woman, desperate as she was, thought that she might possibly be healed as a result. A similar idea is found in the Acts of Apostles where, in the early days of Christianity, sick people were carried into the streets of Jerusalem so that the shadow of Peter, the apostle, could fall on them and heal them (Acts 5.12–16).

The woman clearly believed that there was something divine about the body of Jesus since, as soon as she managed to touch it, she was healed. At the same time, Jesus was aware that some power had left him and he wanted to know why. He turned round to find out who in the crowd had touched him. The disciples found this concern of Jesus absurd when so many people were crowding in on him:

> "You see how the people are crowding you; why do you ask who touched you?"
> (5.31)

Jesus, however, knew that it was important that the woman should identify herself, otherwise she would never be fully healed in mind as well as in body. She had been greatly damaged by the way that the religious laws had cut her off from any contact or fellowship with God's people for such a long time. In Jewish society menstruation made women unclean and removed them from religious worship each month, but for this woman it had gone on much longer. The woman, trembling with fear, knelt at the feet of Jesus and confessed everything to him. Jesus, recognising her faith, told her:

> "My daughter, your faith has made you well. Go in peace, and be healed of your trouble."
> (5.34)

The woman in this story was excluded from all social contact. Women were seen as 'unclean' while they were having their monthly periods. This woman's condition, however, made her continually unclean.

Assessing the miracle

There seems to be more than a little 'magic' in this story, with the woman touching Jesus and being instantly cured. There is no other miracle in the Gospels which has this feature. For Mark, though, it was Jesus himself, rather than any magical power, who healed the woman. The key that unlocked the healing of the woman was her faith, and this is why Jesus brought everything out into the open. Jesus wanted to use her faith as an example to others. This explains the final, impressive statement of Jesus that the woman was not only healed but also saved as well.

One additional thing to notice. By allowing the woman to touch him Jesus had himself, under the Jewish religious laws, become unclean. Jesus had previously done exactly the same thing when he had made himself religiously unclean by touching the leper (1.40–45). By ignoring such laws Jesus was showing the true power of God's kingdom, the power of suffering and the power of love. In this kingdom it was God's will that everyone should be whole.

Key Points

1 The woman thought she could touch Jesus without being noticed and be healed. There is no other healing like this in the Gospels. She believed there was something divine about the body of Jesus.
2 She could only be fully healed – in mind and spirit as well as body – if she identified herself. When she did so Jesus recognised her faith.
3 The faith of the woman was held up as an example to others – she was saved as well as healed.

Work to do

1 Answer each of these questions in your own words:
   a What does Mark say about the medical condition of the woman who tried to be healed by touching the clothes of Jesus?
   b What did the woman say as she approached Jesus, and why do you think she felt like this?
   c What does Mark say about the woman's cure?
   d Why were the disciples surprised when Jesus asked who had touched him from the crowd?
   e How did Jesus know that someone had touched him to seek healing?
2 How did the woman with a flow of blood show that she had faith in Jesus?
3 Describe the stories of the woman with a haemorrhage and the raising of Jairus' daughter.
4 What religious lessons do you think Mark's readers – both at the time he was writing and today – might be expected to draw from the story of the woman healed from her haemorrhage?

In the Glossary

Gospel • Jerusalem • Mark • Peter

The disciples couldn't understand why Jesus was interested in one person touching him when people were crowding all around him.

5.5 The epileptic boy

 Read

Mark 9.14–29

 **Key Question**

How important was the faith of the father in the healing of the epileptic boy?

Mark linked the story of Jesus healing an epileptic boy with the previous episode in which he was transfigured in front of three of his disciples (see Unit 2.2). You may remember that this event ended in some confusion when the disciples failed to understand what was going on. As Peter, James and John came down from the mountain on which the Transfiguration had occurred, they found the other disciples surrounded by an angry crowd. The story that follows is complicated because the effort of the father to have his son healed is interwoven with the failure of the disciples to perform the miracle. It was the failure of the disciples, interpreted by Jesus as a lack of faith, which distressed him most.

The efforts of the father

A group of scribes were involved in the disagreement between the disciples and the child's father. From the beginning of his Gospel Mark has presented the scribes as a group opposed to Jesus, but they disappear from the story quickly here. The child's father explained his anguish to Jesus:

> "Teacher [Rabbi], I brought my son to you, because he has an evil spirit in him and cannot talk. Whenever the spirit attacks him, it throws him to the ground, and he foams at the mouth, grits his teeth, and becomes stiff all over. I asked your disciples to drive the spirit out, but they could not."
> (9.17–18)

Today we would recognise the child's condition as that of epilepsy. In the time of Jesus, though, it was put down to spirit-possession, as were many illnesses. The father had brought the child to Jesus for an exorcism, to have the demon cast out, but he had turned to the disciples for help when Jesus was elsewhere. The disciples, who had already been sent out by Jesus to cast out demons (see Unit 6.3) and had been successful in doing so, were unable to help the child despite their efforts.

The rebuke and the healing

Peter, James and John had just been rebuked for their failure on the mountain, and now the other disciples were being rebuked by Jesus for their lack of faith:

> "How unbelieving you people are!"
> (9.19)

After Jesus had healed the child the disciples asked him why they had been unable to help. He told them:

> "Only prayer can drive this kind out … nothing else can."
> (9.29)

Yet no mention is made by Mark of Jesus praying before healing the child. As the child was brought to Jesus he suffered another epileptic fit. Jesus asked the father how long this had been going on, and was told that the child had always suffered such fits. His cry to Jesus came from the heart:

> "Have pity on us and help us, if you possibly can!"
> (9.22)

The blind Bartimaeus (see Unit 2.12) asked Jesus to show the same emotion towards him – pity. Here Jesus turned the spotlight on the man's faith. Nowhere else in Mark's Gospel is the link between healing and faith spelt out so clearly:

> "Everything is possible for the person who has faith."
> (9.23)

This answer made the man nervous because he wondered if he could meet the demands of Jesus. Did he have enough faith to rise to the challenge put to him? He replied:

> "I do have faith, but not enough. Help me to have more!"
> (9.24)

As the crowd closed in, Jesus ordered the evil spirit to leave the child – and not to return. The last order was important because, in those days, people believed that evil spirits needed to have a home, and could easily return to someone from whom they had been exorcised. The order of Jesus carried great authority, and the evil spirit had no alternative but to leave. He did, however, convulse the boy one last time before he left. The fit was so severe that the child was left on the road as if he were dead. It seemed that all of his life had been squeezed out of him. Jesus, though, took him by the hand and lifted him up.

Key Points

1 This miracle underlines the helplessness of the disciples – which Jesus explained as being due to their lack of faith.
2 The child's father turned to Jesus for help. Jesus rebuked the disciples. The father expressed his deep anguish. Jesus told him that faith in God is the key.
3 Jesus cast the evil spirit out of the child. The spirit convulsed the child before leaving him. The child appeared to be dead but Jesus helped him up.

Work to do

1 a How might a modern writer describe the condition of the child, said to have been possessed by an evil spirit in Mark's Gospel?
  b When Jesus said that the child could only be healed by faith, what did his father ask for?
  c Describe what happened to the boy after his father's cry for help.
2 Describe the healing of the epileptic boy. Explain what this story teaches about faith, prayer and commitment.
3 In what ways was the healing of the epileptic boy like the healing of the paralysed man in Mark 2.1–5?

In the Glossary

Disciple • Exorcism • Gospel • James • John • Mark • Peter • Rabbi • Scribe • Transfiguration

The incident of the epileptic boy being healed by Jesus underlines the importance of prayer for all Christians – young and old.

Read

**Mark
1.16–28;
2.13–17**

Key Question

How did the call of Jesus to the first disciples set the tone for the rest of his ministry?

In the time of Jesus disciples usually attached themselves to a rabbi. Jesus, though, took the initiative and invited disciples to follow him.

Discipleship (following Jesus) is a very important theme in Mark's Gospel. After his account of the baptism and temptation of Jesus (1.9–13) Mark moves on to describe how Jesus calls two sets of brothers to follow him. The brothers are carefully identified by Mark, since three of them – Peter (Simon), James and John – were to become the closest confidants of Jesus during his ministry. All four of them were fishermen, but Jesus called them to leave their old life behind them and become his disciples.

Simon and Andrew (1.16–18)

Jesus found all four fishermen working on the shore of the Sea of Galilee which was the centre of a busy fishing industry. To the first two of them, Simon and Andrew, Jesus said:

> "Come with me, and I will teach you to catch men."
> (1.17)

For Jesus to call disciples in this way was highly unusual, since disciples always made their own way to follow a teacher (rabbi) – not vice versa. For Mark the significance of the incident lay in the response of the disciples to Jesus and his call:

> "At once they left their nets and went with him."
> (1.18)

The men had to leave all that they had to follow Jesus. In return, Jesus promised them a part in the task of proclaiming the coming of God's kingdom on earth. The drawing of people into that kingdom was the whole purpose behind the life of Jesus on earth. Preaching the Good News (the Gospel) rather than healing or driving out demons lay at the heart of the ministry of Jesus. Miracles of healing and exorcism were only signs of God's kingdom, but they were not what the kingdom was really about.

James and John (1.19–20)

Jesus found James and John, the sons of Zebedee, when they were preparing their nets for their next fishing expedition at the lakeside. We are simply told that Jesus 'called' them. Again the normal arrangement between rabbi and pupil was broken. James and John left their father and followed ('came after') Jesus.

The word 'disciple' is not used of any of these fishermen, although the idea of leaving everything and 'following' is an important part of discipleship. It was only when Matthew was called to follow Jesus (see below) that his followers were called 'disciples' for the first time. Simon, Andrew, James and John responded to Jesus without knowing that he was God's Messiah. Indeed, they could not have known much about him at all. Slowly, though, as they found out more about Jesus, so the cost of being a disciple (see 8.34–38; 10.24–31) impressed itself upon them, as it did on the other disciples.

Levi (2.14)

We are not sure who Levi was, but there is good reason to identify him with Matthew, one of the twelve disciples chosen by Jesus (3.18). His work as a tax-collector made him an 'outcast' in the eyes of his fellow-Jews. The taxes collected went to the much-hated puppet of Rome, Herod Antipas, but the collectors were all Jews. Their wealth came from the extra money they charged the people over and above that demanded by Rome. Levi's position in society was much the same as that of the 'loan-shark' today. There was also the added stigma of him being a 'collaborator' working, as he did, for the enemy, the Romans.

Vocation

Christians today speak of a 'calling' or 'vocation'. People who feel themselves called to the priesthood, or to life in a religious order, speak of having a vocation. Roman Catholic priests take on the 'calling' to live a celibate life, whilst monks and nuns take the three-fold vow of poverty, chastity and obedience. In a wider sense all Christians believe that they have a vocation to be a disciple. For most this means that they are 'called' to serve God through their family and working life.

James and John, fishermen brothers, left their boat and nets behind to become disciples of Jesus.

Key Points

1 Jesus hand-picked each of his twelve disciples.
2 In Mark's Gospel we discover how he called five of the Twelve. Four of them were fishermen and the fifth, Levi, was a tax-collector who worked for the Romans.
3 The disciples had a vocation (calling) to follow Jesus. In the Christian Church priests, monks and nuns are also said to have a vocation.

Work to do

1 What did Jesus say to Simon and Andrew when he called them to be disciples? What did he mean?
2 In describing the call of James and John, Mark drew a contrast between the two fishermen who left all to follow Jesus and the hired servants who stayed behind to run the business. What lesson do you think he wanted his readers to learn from this?

3 The first four disciples who followed Jesus in Mark's Gospel were all fishermen. Can you suggest any reason for this, or was it pure coincidence?
4 When Jesus was criticised for eating with outcasts he replied:

"People who are well do not need a doctor, but only those who are sick. I have not come to call respectable people, but outcasts."
(2.17)

a Who criticised Jesus for eating with outcasts and sinners?
b Why do you think Jesus often ate with the outcasts of society?
c What does the reply of Jesus suggest about the reason why he came to earth?

In the Glossary

Andrew • Disciple • Gospel • Herod Antipas • James • John • Kingdom of God • Matthew • Messiah • Monk • Nun • Peter • Priest • Rabbi • Vocation

6.2 Choosing the Twelve

Read

Mark 3.13–19

Key Question

What is significant about the twelve disciples that Jesus chose, and what did he give them to do?

We know from the other Gospels that Jesus went up into a mountain (or hill) to pray before choosing his twelve closest friends, or disciples. The Gospel writers wanted their readers to know that even Jesus, the Son of God, needed to spend time praying to God before making the important decisions in his ministry. We shall come across this again in the Garden of Gethsemane when Jesus struggled to accept the truth – that he was shortly to meet a violent death (see Unit 3.1). There he spent much of the night in prayer.

Jesus attracted many followers early in his ministry, and he needed to select a small group from this large crowd. Mark called this group the 'apostles' ('those who are sent') until Jesus sent them out on a preaching and healing mission (6.7–13). After this he called them disciples. They were called 'apostles' again after the day of Pentecost.

The work of the disciples

Mark tells us that Jesus chose his twelve disciples for three main reasons:

1 To be with him. From this time onwards they were to be his closest human friends. He was to spend much of his time teaching them about the Kingdom of God so that they could, after his death, pass the same message on to others. From this group of twelve Jesus chose just three disciples – Peter, James and John – to share his most intimate moments, such as the Transfiguration (9.2–13) and the Garden of Gethsemane agony (14.32–42).

2 To preach. They were to spread the Good News (Gospel) about the Kingdom of God. Although the healing work of Jesus and his disciples was important, it was not at the centre of his mission. Jesus, above everything else, had come to tell people about entering God's kingdom. Through the disciples this responsibility was passed on to all members of the Church. The same responsibility is carried by every Christian in the world today.

The mission of the disciples to preach, teach and heal was handed down to the Christian Church.

3 To drive out demons. The disciples shared with Jesus the authority to fight a battle against all the powers of darkness, and to heal people. Many Christians believe that the power to heal remains with the Church today.

The Twelve

The choice of twelve disciples was significant to all Jewish followers of Jesus. The Jewish nation had been based on the twelve tribes, which were named after the sons of Jacob. Now the new Israel (the Christian Church) had replaced the Jewish nation in Mark's mind, and was based on the teaching of the twelve disciples. Little is known about some of the disciples that Jesus chose, but some information is available about most of them:

● Two belonged to groups who were hated, or feared, by most of the Jewish population. Matthew was a hated tax-gatherer working for the Romans, while

Simon was a Zealot (patriot) actively plotting for the overthrow of Roman control in Palestine. To have been a genuine Zealot Simon must have been, at some time, a man of violence.

- Another Simon became the leader of the disciples and of the early Church after the death of Jesus. The name of this Simon was changed by Jesus to Peter ('the rock'). It was the same Peter who promised that he would follow Jesus to death – but who ended up denying that he even knew him (see Unit 3.2).
- James and John were given the nickname 'Boanerges' ('Sons of Thunder') because of the violence of their temper.
- Judas was the disciple who finally betrayed Jesus and then committed suicide. His name, Iscariot, probably indicates that he came from Judea, whereas all the other disciples came from Galilee. This may explain why he was an 'outsider' amongst the Twelve. He was the treasurer of the group, and he used this position to siphon off money for his own purposes.

Discipleship in the Church today

The Roman Catholic Church believes that its bishops follow in a direct line from the disciples of Jesus, and so carry their authority. Other Churches do not agree with these claims, but they do believe that the responsibility of the Church today is the same as that given to the original disciples. It is to preach the Gospel (Good News) of God's kingdom and to continue the fight of Jesus against evil and suffering.

Key Points

1 Jesus chose twelve disciples to be with him, to preach the good news and to drive out demons.
2 Just as the nation of Israel was built on twelve tribes, so the Christian Church was built on the twelve disciples.
3 Matthew and Simon worked for two hated groups in Palestine – the Zealots and the Romans. Judas betrayed Jesus. James and John had violent tempers. Peter was the outstanding leader among the disciples.

Roman Catholics believe that the authority of the disciples was handed down to bishops – the leaders of the Church today.

Work to do

1 Mark tells us:

"he chose twelve, whom he named apostles. 'I have chosen you to be with me,' he told them. 'I will also send you out to preach, and you will have authority to drive out demons.'" (3.14–15)

a What does the word 'apostle' mean, and why was this an appropriate name for the disciples?
b Why do you think that Jesus chose a small group from all those following him, and what did he expect of them?
c Following Jesus clearly turned the lives of the first disciples upside down. In what ways do you think becoming a Christian disciple today might make a difference to a person's life?
2 Jesus had clear reasons in his mind for needing to choose twelve disciples to accompany him. What were those reasons?

In the Glossary

Apostle • Disciple • James • John • Judas Iscariot • Kingdom of God • Mark • Pentecost • Peter • Roman Catholic Church • Transfiguration • Zealots

6.3 Sending out the Twelve

Read

Mark
6.7–13

Key Question

Why did Jesus send out his disciples, and what did he expect them to do?

The action of Jesus in sending out his disciples to preach and heal those in need marked a new stage in his mission. Up until now the work of introducing God's kingdom had been totally in his own hands, but now some part of that mission was given over to his disciples. The twelve disciples went out and told the people to 'turn away from their sins' (6.12), the same message that had been preached previously by John the Baptist (1.4) and Jesus himself (1.15). They went out in pairs so that they could support one another, and the early Church continued this practice after Jesus left the earth (Acts 8.14; 13.1–2).

Men with a mission

Mark's account often has a sense of urgency, which helps to explain the nature of the disciples' mission. The disciples were to work alongside Jesus in bringing in God's kingdom, and there was no time to lose. They were to be men in a hurry and nothing was to interfere with their mission. Their mission was urgent. For this reason they were only to take light equipment with them – a staff, tunic and sandals – but no bread, purse or even a small coin in their belt. Those engaged in God's work must not be fussy about food or accommodation, since their message is one of life or death for their hearers.

It was assumed that the disciples would receive warm hospitality along the way, since this was an important Jewish obligation extended to all travellers. They were to stay in the same house in a village until their mission there was completed. If they were rejected, however, and not able to find anywhere to stay, they were to shake the dust of that village off their feet and move on. Jewish people would have understood this instruction. Each time a Jew returned to Israel (holy land) from Gentile territory (unholy land), he shook the dust from his feet. Mark says that the action, which was encouraged by Jesus, was to be a 'warning to them' (6.11). The warning would be of God's final judgement unless they repented and welcomed the Gospel.

Apart from preaching that the people should repent of their sins, Marks tells us that the disciples on their mission drove out demons and healed people.

Driving out demons

This was something that Jesus frequently did to show that the Kingdom of God had arrived. On two occasions we read that he healed men with evil spirits (1.21–28; 5.1–20), but this was obviously just the tip of the iceberg. Mark tells us that Jesus drove out many demons in one town alone (1.34).

Healing the people

The practice of rubbing olive oil into people to heal them (6.13) is not mentioned elsewhere in Mark, or in any of the other Gospels, although there are many instances of people being healed without oil being involved. We do know, however, that it was a Jewish practice and widely used in the early Church (see information box). Probably the later practice is reflected in the words of Mark here.

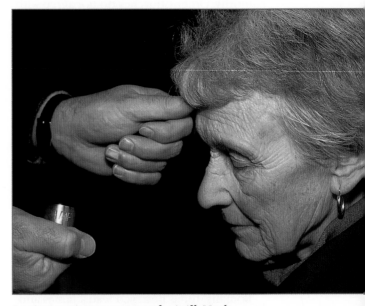

A priest anoints a woman who is ill. Mark mentions a similar practice being carried out by the disciples of Jesus.

A Salvation Army band holds an open-air service. They are obeying the instruction of Jesus to preach the Gospel to all people.

Discipleship today

Disciples of Jesus today still try to carry out the same work as that given by Jesus to his disciples. They try:
- to preach the Gospel;
- to care for the sick;
- to feed the hungry;
- to fight against evil and injustice wherever it is found.

Christians do this in the area in which they live. Some Christians, however, go to other countries where they believe that God has 'called' them to work as missionaries. Christians also support and finance the work of organisations like Christian Aid, Oxfam and CAFOD which respond to the needs of many people in different countries.

Key Points

1 Jesus sending his disciples out to preach marked a new stage in his ministry. Until now he had done all the teaching, preaching and healing.
2 The disciples were not to waste any time and were to travel light. This underlined the urgency of their work. They were to accept hospitality but move on if it was not offered.
3 The Twelve were to cast out demons and heal those with evil spirits.
4 Christians today try to carry out the same work, including caring for the sick and feeding the hungry.

For your Information

Giving advice to Christians in the church around 55 CE, James tells them:

"Is there anyone who is ill? He should send for the church elders, who will pray for him and rub olive-oil on him in the name of the Lord. This prayer made in faith will heal the sick person; the Lord will restore him to health."

Work to do

1 a When Jesus sent out his twelve disciples he gave them some advice. State two instructions that he gave them.
  b How were the disciples sent out, and what authority were they given?
  c What were the disciples to do if a village did not welcome them?
2 Why do you think that people in the time of Jesus believed in demons and evil spirits? Do you think that such a belief has any place in modern life?
3 What is the link between Mark 6.13 and James 5.14–15?

In the Glossary

Gentile • Gospel • James • John the Baptist • Kingdom of God

83

6.4 The nature and cost of discipleship

 Read

Mark 8.34–38

 **Key Question**

What, according to Jesus, is the cost which has to be paid by anyone who would be his disciple?

As his ministry began to draw towards its close Jesus tried to warn his disciples that he was going to be brutally put to death. After one such warning (8.31–32) Peter could not accept that any such thing would happen to Jesus, but Jesus strongly rebuked his disciple. He then went on to spell out to everyone listening the cost that had to be paid by anyone who seriously wanted to be one of his followers.

The cost of being a disciple

Jesus explained that his own destiny was to suffer and die. That is why he came to earth in the first place. Any disciple of Jesus must be prepared to do the same. This warning was addressed to the disciples, the wider audience of people listening – and to the later Christian Church. By the time that Mark was writing, around 65 CE, the Christian Church was undergoing its first persecution. The message that he was sending to the Church was blunt – they should not have expected anything else but suffering, persecution and possible death.

Jesus knew that he would be crucified. By this time the opposition to him was building up and there could be no other possible outcome. This is why he spoke to those listening in terms of each disciple 'taking up their own cross' and following in his footsteps. Even if Jesus was not forecasting the actual death of his followers he was asking them to give up their security and their own interests, which might, in many cases, lead to death itself.

Losing and saving life

These words of Jesus led him to reflect on the true meaning of discipleship. He stated it in the form of a paradox. Anyone who loses his life for the sake of the Gospel of Jesus will end up by saving it in the life to come. Nothing matters more than saving one's soul. It is better to lose everything and save one's soul than to gain the whole world. If anyone is ashamed of Jesus, and his words, in this world then the Son of Man (Jesus) will be ashamed of him in the world to come when he returns to earth with God's angels.

It is not clear whether Jesus was talking about the arrival of God's kingdom in the lifetime of those listening. If he was, then the reward that he was promising his followers has clearly failed to materialise. He did not return to Earth. It is more likely that Jesus was referring to an event which was ultimately certain, but which had no time limit. Sometime in the future God's kingdom will be set up on earth. Jesus himself did not know when this would happen. The only certain thing is that it will happen in God's time.

Jesus drew a parallel between having to carry his own cross on the way to execution and his disciples each having to carry their own crosses.

James was one of the disciples who gave his life for his faith.

Key Points

1 Jesus tried to warn his disciples that he would be put to death. They did not understand what he was saying and on one occasion Peter could not accept that this would happen to Jesus.

2 Jesus promised that his disciples and followers would suffer in the same way that he was going to do. For many that could involve losing their lives.

3 To draw a parallel with his own death Jesus spoke of his followers taking up their own cross.

Work to do

1 Jesus spoke plainly to his disciples about the cost that might have to be paid by those who follow him.
   a How did he describe the possible cost to be paid by each disciple?
   b With what did Jesus draw a parallel to explain the sufferings of his disciples?

2 Write a paragraph describing the true cost of Christian discipleship.

6.5 The rewards of discipleship

Read

10.28–31

Key Question

What are the rewards that Jesus promised to those who left everything to follow him?

Jesus had an extended conversation with a wealthy young Jew who wanted to know how he could become a follower (see Unit 4.3). He concluded that the man's wealth was the major barrier standing in the way of him entering into the Kingdom of God. Jesus also used the encounter to spell out the rewards which were given to those who prized doing God's will above everything else in life.

The rewards of discipleship

The problem for the young man was his wealth. This was a comment that astonished his hearers, especially his disciples, who believed that the young man was well placed to enter God's kingdom ahead of almost anyone else. Jesus used their astonishment to underline the basic truth about Christian discipleship – the true disciple will place God and his demands on them ahead of all family relationships. This includes the relationship of husband with wife and vice versa, together with the relationship that exists between parents and children.

This was (and is) asking a great deal. Certainly the Twelve were expected to leave behind their closest relationships when Jesus called them to follow him. Now Jesus tells them that those who have given up everything for his sake will be rewarded. He even implied that they would be rewarded both in this present age and in the age to come. The reference to a reward in this present age implies that even though they have given up their family they will experience a new 'family' and 'community' – the Church. In this new community existing values will be turned upside down. That is why the very poor widow who gave her last coins to God was so highly commended by Jesus (see Unit 6.6). Her sense of priorities was absolutely right – and she was rewarded by God for it.

Christians and the example of Jesus

Modern Christians believe that, just like the disciples of old, they are called to follow the example that Jesus set. They spend time discovering the teachings of Jesus from the Bible and trying to put those teachings into practice. Jesus is their example of someone who lived his whole life in the light of the demands of the Kingdom of God. As Jesus reminded them, in God's kingdom the first will be last and the last first.

Many people found the demand of Jesus that he should be placed ahead of all family relationships and ties very difficult to accept. There are indications that many would-be disciples were put off from following Jesus by this demand.

Key Points

1 Jesus spelled out the demands of Christian discipleship and the rewards offered to the faithful disciple.
2 The true disciple will place God and God's demands ahead of the most important of their human relationships.
3 The disciple may lose the closest of human relationships but becomes a member of God's family and the new Christian community to which he or she belongs.
4 The poor widow is a good example of someone who places God ahead of everything, and everyone, else.

Work to do

1 What did Jesus say to underline his teaching that the true disciple will place God above everything else in life – no matter how important it might be?
2 a Describe two ways in which Christian disciples today might show the important place that God occupies in their lives.
  b Why do you think that Christians hold up Jesus as the supreme example of someone who placed the demands of God's kingdom ahead of everything else in their life?

Jesus implied that the Church was the new 'family' for those who had become Christians.

6.6 The poor widow

 Read

Mark
12.41–44

 **Key
Question**

**Why did
Jesus hold
up the poor
widow as a
great
example to
all Christian
disciples?**

On more than one occasion in Mark's Gospel Jesus had a bitter exchange of views with a group described as being 'scribes'. These people were responsible for copying out the Jewish Scriptures and for passing their knowledge of the Scriptures on to the ordinary people. There were certainly bitter exchanges between the disciples of Jesus and the Jewish leaders in the days of the early Church, and these are reflected in this incident in Mark. The scribes were responsible for the welfare of the widows and their children in Jewish society, and Jesus appears to accuse them here of falling down on this responsibility.

The poor widow

Jesus drew a stark contrast between the behaviour of the scribes and that of the poor widow who gave her last few coins to the Temple treasury in Jerusalem (12.42). The two copper coins that she dropped in were worth about a penny. Her gift has been estimated to have been worth about one sixty-fourth of a denarius, a day's wage for a very poorly paid labourer. Yet, in drawing attention to the woman's actions, Jesus made it clear that she had, in spiritual terms, given far more than all the people who put much larger sums of money into the treasury. They had given just a little of their total wealth but she had put in all that she had to live on. Her gift involved true sacrifice, while that of the others had not.

The action of the poor widow brings together the two commandments that Jesus had just been speaking about (see Unit 4.5). By her selfless act the woman had shown that she really loved God with her whole heart, soul, mind and strength. She could not have loved God any more. She also gave her all so that others were able to benefit from her actions. Jesus believed, and taught, that people show their real love for God when they act from the heart. It was this that lay at the heart of most of the disputes that Jesus had with the religious authorities and which dogged his ministry from beginning to end. As he constantly pointed out, it is possible to keep all the requirements of the

The scrolls of the Law in a synagogue. Jesus said that the poor widow was keeping both the letter and the meaning of the Law.

Law – and yet to disregard both God and the requirements of one's fellow human beings.

Today, as then, these words of Jesus stand at the very heart of the Christian faith. The heart of that faith lies in:
- loving God with one's whole being;
- serving and meeting the needs of one's fellow human beings just as Jesus did throughout his ministry.

Key Points

1 Jesus drew a contrast between the behaviour of the Jewish leaders and that of a poor widow who placed all that she had in the Temple treasury.

2 Jesus praised the woman because her gift involved real sacrifice, while the others only gave out of their wealth.

3 By behaving as she did the woman was showing a real love for God and a willingness to give to meet the needs of her fellow human beings.

In the Glossary

Jerusalem • Scribe • Temple

Work to do

1 a What did Jesus see as he was standing by the Temple treasury?
  b Why was the small gift of the woman so significant to Jesus?
  c Which two commandments did the woman show that she was obeying by her actions?

2 By looking up the following references and combining them with the story of the poor widow, describe what Jesus taught about the importance and danger of riches:
  a Luke 12.33;
  b Luke 16.9;
  c Luke 19.8;
  d Luke 12.13–21.

Jesus placed as much emphasis upon helping fellow human beings as he did on worshipping God, as the incident of the poor widow shows.

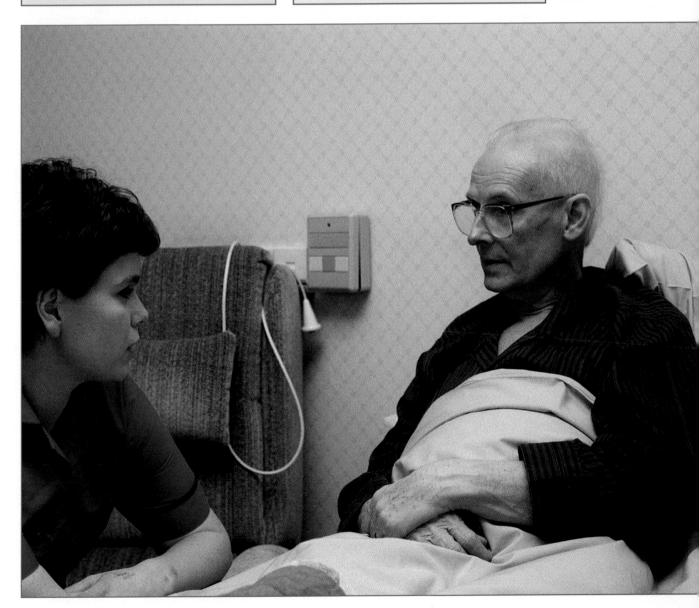

Key Question

What is the Sabbath day, and why was it such an important part of Jewish religion in the time of Jesus?

The Sabbath day is the weekly day of rest observed by Jews from sunset on Friday until nightfall on Saturday – a period of some 25 hours. Observing the Sabbath is the oldest of all Jewish religious traditions, going back to the time of Moses.

The importance of the Sabbath

Apart from its antiquity in the Jewish faith there are three main reasons for the importance of the Sabbath day:

1 God created the world in six days and rested on the seventh. In the story of creation we are told that:

> "He [God] blessed the seventh day and set it apart as a special day, because by that day he had completed his creation and stopped working."
> (Genesis 2.3)

2 The Sabbath day is the only festival, weekly or annual, mentioned in the Ten Commandments:

> "Observe the Sabbath and keep it holy. You have six days in which to do your work, but the seventh day is a day of rest dedicated to me. On that day no one is to work . . . In six days I, the Lord, made the earth, the sky, the sea, and everything in them, but on the seventh day I rested. That is why I, the Lord, blessed the Sabbath and made it holy."
> (Exodus 20.8–11)

God later spoke to Moses and told him that the Sabbath day was holy, a sign to show that:

> "I, the Lord, have made you my own people."
> (Exodus 31.13)

Anyone who worked on that day was to be put to death!

3 The Sabbath day was linked with the release of the Jews from Egyptian slavery (Deuteronomy 5.15). This event, called the Exodus, was the most important demonstration of God's power in Jewish history. The Sabbath day therefore linked the two greatest events in Jewish history – the creation of the world and the Exodus.

Observing the Sabbath

For a long time keeping the Sabbath day was so important that Jewish warriors preferred to die at the hands of their enemies rather than fight on this day. By the time of Jesus, though, the rabbis had ruled that the preservation of life – one's own or that of others – overruled all Sabbath observance. Warriors could defend themselves, while Jews could act if human or animal life was threatened on the Sabbath day.

There were 39 categories of work that were forbidden on the Sabbath day. These included sowing and reaping, ploughing, threshing, winnowing, baking, tying a knot, hunting, slaughtering, salting the skin of an animal, cutting up an animal, writing two or more letters of the alphabet, building a house, lighting or putting out a fire, striking a hammer or carrying something from one place to another. More categories of 'work' were added by the Pharisees to make sure that no one broke the Sabbath laws by accident. Jesus objected more to these extra rules than to the laws themselves.

Jesus and the Sabbath day

Jesus emphasised the importance of meeting human need rather than keeping the Sabbath regulations. The Jewish laws, for example, allowed medical action on the Sabbath day if a person's life was in danger, but Jesus went further than this. He healed the man with the withered hand (3.1–6), exorcised demons (1.21–28) and performed other miracles on the Sabbath day although the lives of the people were not at risk. (We will look at several examples of this in Units 7.2–7.4.) Jesus summed up his own attitude towards the Sabbath day and human need in his answer to the Pharisees when they criticised his disciples for picking ears of corn on the holy day:

> "The Sabbath was made for the good of man; man was not made for the Sabbath."
> (2.27)

For your Information

In Mark's Gospel:

- Jesus is said to have participated in Sabbath services on three occasions (1.21; 3.1; 6.2).

- Sabbath customs are noted on two occasions – the people wait until the Sabbath is over before carrying the sick to Jesus (1.32), and the women wait until the Sabbath has finished before anointing the body of Jesus with spices (16.1).

- Jesus sometimes healed on the Sabbath day without any objections being raised (1.21–28, 29–31).

Key Points

1 The Sabbath day has always been a very important Jewish celebration. It is a weekly festival. It remembers the creation of the world by God. It also celebrates the greatest event in Jewish history – the Exodus.
2 The Sabbath day was kept strictly as a day of rest. It was, though, lawful to work if human or animal life was in danger.
3 Jesus emphasised that human need was more important than the strict observance of the Sabbath day.

Sabbath worship, then as now, centred around the home and started with a family meal.

Work to do

1 Write down three pieces of information about the Jewish Sabbath day.
2 Give two reasons why Jews keep the Sabbath as a special day.
3 Explain how the attitude of Jesus towards the Sabbath day was different to that of the Jewish leaders.
4 Jesus said:

"The Sabbath was made for the good of man; man was not made for the Sabbath."

Explain what you think Jesus was trying to say about the Sabbath.

The interior of a modern synagogue. The main Sabbath service takes place on the Saturday morning and involves the whole family.

In the Glossary

Disciple • Exodus • Moses • Pharisees • Sabbath day • Ten Commandments

7.2 The man with an evil spirit

Read

Mark
1.21–28

Key Question

What was the importance of Jesus' healing of the man with an evil spirit?

Jesus spent much of his early ministry in and around the town of Capernaum (1.21; 2.1; 3.1; 9.33) and other places dotted around the shores of the Lake of Galilee (1.9; 2.13; 3.7; 4.1). At the beginning of his Gospel, Mark tells us that Jesus entered the synagogue in Capernaum on the Sabbath day and began to preach. The ruler of a synagogue often invited important visitors to take part in services. The participation of Jesus in an act of Sabbath worship shows that his fellow-Jews were beginning to recognise him as a rabbi (teacher) although he had not received any formal training. This acceptance, however, was not to last long. Soon Jesus was to find that the synagogues were closed to him and his message. He was then forced to teach in the open air, as he usually did, or in the houses of his followers.

Jesus in the synagogue

Mark tells us nothing about the teaching of Jesus in the synagogue on this occasion, although Luke does in his parallel account (4.31–37). Mark's interest is instead in the miracle which followed when Jesus encountered a man with an evil spirit. Before this, however, he described the effect that the teaching of Jesus had on those listening to him:

> "The people who heard him were amazed at the way he taught, for he wasn't like the teachers of the Law; instead, he taught with authority."
> (1.22)

Later (6.1–6) Jesus was rejected by those listening to him in a synagogue, but on this occasion he received a positive welcome from the people. The authority of his teaching is compared favourably with that of the scribes. The hostility between Jesus and the teachers of the Law (the scribes) begins in Mark's Gospel at a very early stage and continues to the end. They later enter into a dispute with him over the forgiveness of sins (2.5–7), as well as putting his power down to Beelzebul, the prince of the demons (3.22).

The amazement of the people at the teaching of Jesus, a reaction totally different from that of the scribes, is frequently found in Mark's Gospel (1.22; 1.27; 1.32). Time after time it is the ordinary people, and not the religious leaders, who respond favourably to Jesus. This is a reminder to Christians today that they have a responsibility to offer the Christian message to everyone.

The miracle

Unlike some of his later miracles, such as the healing of the man with the withered arm (see Unit 7.4), the fact that this miracle took place on the Sabbath day is not particularly important in Mark's description. This may have been due to the absence of the

This Jewish stained glass window contains some symbols of Jewish worship.

Pharisees, scribes and Herodians while the miracle was being performed. Later criticism of breaking the Sabbath laws came almost exclusively from members of these groups.

A man with an unclean spirit suddenly appeared to challenge the authority of Jesus by screaming at him:

> "What do you want with us, Jesus of Nazareth? Are you here to destroy us? I know who you are – you are God's holy messenger!"
> (1.24)

The title given to Jesus by the evil spirit, 'God's holy messenger', reminds us of the voice from heaven at his baptism which called him 'God's Son' (1.11). Jesus belonged to God in a special way – he was the Messiah. We have already learned that Jesus spent 40 days in the wilderness after his baptism, being tempted by the Devil. Now, for the second time in Mark's Gospel, Jesus was brought into direct conflict with the powers of darkness and evil, who challenged the authority which was the basis of his ministry.

Jesus showed his authority over these powers by ordering the evil spirit to come out of the man. The spirit shook the man, gave a loud cry and left him (1.26). For a second time the people are said to be 'amazed'. This time they are staggered by Jesus' power over the evil spirits, who take their orders from him and obey his words. The exorcism convinced the people not only of the power of Jesus but also of the authority of his words. The news of him, and his work, spread like wildfire through the whole region of Galilee.

Key Points

1 On more than one occasion Jesus took part in Sabbath worship in his nearest synagogue. He soon found, however, that he was not welcome in any synagogue. He began to teach in the open air.
2 On one visit to a synagogue he spoke in the service and amazed the people with the authority with which he spoke. The scribes were very hostile towards him.
3 Jesus performed more than one miracle on the Sabbath day. When he healed a man with an evil spirit on the Sabbath day he came into sharp conflict with the powers of evil.

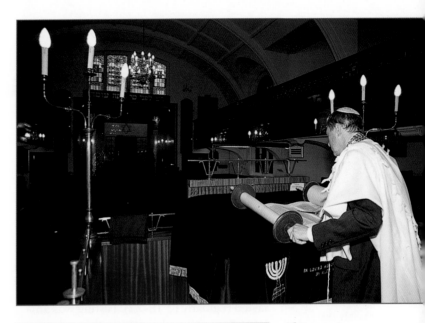

This man is reading from a scroll of the Jewish scriptures, just as Jesus did in the synagogue.

Work to do

1 a Explain, in your own words, just what happened when Jesus encountered a man with an evil spirit in the synagogue at Capernaum.
  b Why were the people amazed when Jesus cast the evil spirit out of the man?
2 Although this miracle was performed on the Sabbath day, this does not seem to have been an important issue. Can you suggest one reason for this?
3 After Jesus cast the evil spirit out of the man, the people in the crowd began saying to each other:

> "What is this? Is it some new kind of teaching? The man has authority to give orders to the evil spirits and they obey him!"
> (1.27)

What were the two kinds of authority shown by Jesus in this incident that so impressed the people?

In the Glossary

Devil • Exorcism • Gospel • Mark • Messiah • Pharisees • Rabbi • Sabbath day • Scribe • Synagogue

7.3 A dispute about the Sabbath day

 Read

Mark 2.18–22; 2.23–28

 **Key Question**

How did Jesus deal with the objection from the Pharisees about the behaviour of his disciples on the Sabbath day?

Two complaints about the behaviour of the disciples were made early in the ministry of Jesus: they didn't fast regularly, and they broke the Sabbath laws.

The question about fasting

The unorthodox behaviour of Jesus and his disciples puzzled many ordinary people. They wanted to know why the disciples did not follow the example of the disciples of John the Baptist and the Pharisees who fasted regularly (2.18–22). Fasting was an important spiritual activity in the early Church, and this question reflects that importance. Fasting is still practised in many Churches, such as the Orthodox Church, and is often used as a form of spiritual preparation for important festivals such as Easter.

Mark agreed that fasting would be important for Christians when Jesus had left the earth, but not while he was there with his disciples (2.20). As Jesus put it, the guests at a wedding feast do not fast while the bridegroom is with them (2.19). They only begin to fast when the feast is over and the bridegroom has gone away.

Mark goes on to describe two brief parables to show that the old and the new ways do not mix. If a new piece of cloth is sewn to an old garment to mend it, Jesus argued, it will shrink when it is washed and produce a larger hole than the original tear (2.21). Similarly, if new wine is poured into old wineskins to store it, the old skins will burst and the wine will be lost (2.22). New wine must be stored in new wineskins. The suggestion seems to be that the new way brought by Jesus could not simply be attached to the old religion which depended on man-made laws and regulations.

Mark wants us to remember these parables when we come to the next section, which describes how the disciples were picked up for 'breaking' the Sabbath laws. The laws surrounding the Sabbath day were not important in the new way that Jesus had come to bring – the way which allowed people to enter the Kingdom of God for themselves.

The Lord of the Sabbath

So to the controversy with the Pharisees about the Sabbath day. The disciples walked through the cornfields on the Sabbath day, and picked some ears of corn as they went. Everyone did this in Palestine and it was not illegal. Jesus could have pointed his critics to Deuteronomy 23.25, where picking a few ears of corn, as opposed to harvesting, was permitted on the Sabbath day. It was the interpretation of this by the scribes, who turned such a simple activity into a form of work, which created the problem.

In responding to the criticism of the Pharisees, Jesus appealed to the example of the much-loved Jewish king, David. He reminded his accusers of the time when the king, and those with him, were hungry and entered the house of God to eat the special bread which was offered to God (1 Samuel 21.1–6). His listeners would know that, by custom, only the priests were allowed to eat this bread. In fact, this story from the Jewish Scriptures had nothing whatever to do with what was and what was not allowed on the Sabbath day. Rather, it demonstrated that human need was far more important than any customs, rules and regulations.

Jesus left his accusers with a memorable saying, attached to the story, which expressed his real attitude to the Sabbath day:

> "The Sabbath was made for the good of man; man was not made for the Sabbath. So the Son of Man is Lord even of the Sabbath."
> (2.27–28)

We do not know whether the saying was part of the original incident, or whether Mark placed it here because it seemed to be particularly appropriate. The saying, though, does underline what Jesus has been saying all along – the Sabbath day is a blessing only if it meets the needs of ordinary men and women. If it places a millstone around their necks and weighs them down, then they are better off without it. Such a message was hardly calculated to appeal to his Jewish readers.

This is a Jewish place of worship – a synagogue. Many of the laws surrounding the Sabbath day are still in place for Jews today.

The Son of Man

Look back at Unit 2.3 for details about the Son of Man. Here, to underline what has been said about human laws, the saying emphasises that the Son of Man, Jesus, is greater than all such laws. This is the second saying in a short space of time about the Son of Man. In the first (2.10) the Son of Man is said to have power on earth to forgive sins, as Jesus showed when he healed the paralysed man. Now the Son of Man is the Lord of the Sabbath day (2.28). Jesus has shown that human need overrides the demands of the Law. Respecting the Sabbath is part of that Law. Since Jesus is the authoritative interpreter of the Law, the Son of Man is also Lord of the Sabbath.

Key Points

1 The disciples were criticised for not fasting regularly. Jesus said that fasting belonged to the old religion. It was not required in the new faith that he had brought.
2 The disciples were criticised for picking corn on the Sabbath day. Jesus pointed out that King David had broken the law when need required it.
3 Mark's Gospel says that the Son of Man, Jesus, is greater than all human laws. He has power to forgive sins and is greater than the Sabbath laws.

Work to do

1 Imagine that you are a Pharisee at the time of Jesus. Write a little about what you believe, and why you believe that the laws about keeping the Sabbath day holy and special are necessary.
2 a What is the Sabbath?
  b Why was Jesus concerned to maintain that human beings are more important than the Sabbath day, and not the other way round?
  c Who was the 'Son of Man' and why did Jesus maintain that he was 'Lord, even of the Sabbath'?
3 Why do you think that the Pharisees criticised Jesus for allowing his disciples to pluck ears of corn on the Sabbath day?

In the Glossary

Disciple • Easter • Fasting • John the Baptist • Mark • Orthodox Church • Parable • Pharisees • Sabbath day • Scribe • Son of Man

7.4 The man with the withered arm

Read

Mark
3.1–6

Key Question

What question did Jesus put to the religious authorities in Capernaum, and why did it place them in an impossible position?

The opponents of Jesus were looking for another opportunity to accuse him of paying no regard to the Sabbath day. The first healing in Mark's Gospel on the Sabbath day (1.21–28) had led to the widespread amazement of the people. Jesus, they decided, was not like the scribes, the Jewish religious teachers of the day, since his divine authority forced even the evil spirits to obey him.

Now, though, in a short space of time the situation had changed dramatically. Since that miracle, the religious leaders had worked hard to change the minds of the people about Jesus. A general antagonism towards him, and his work, had begun to grow among them. When Jesus arrived in the synagogue in Capernaum (3.1–6) there were many people just waiting to catch him out. As Mark tells us (3.2), people were watching to see if he performed another miracle on the Sabbath so that they could accuse him of doing wrong.

The miracle

The convenient presence of a man with a withered arm in the synagogue on the Sabbath appears to have been a 'set-up'. The religious leaders were trying to provoke Jesus into performing a miracle on the holy day. Jesus did not disappoint them. The man with the withered arm was made to stand up in front of everyone in the synagogue, and was called by Jesus out to the front so that everyone could see his condition. Turning to the people crowded into the building, Jesus asked them the crucial question:

> "What does our Law allow us to do on the Sabbath? To help or to harm? To save a man's life or to destroy it?"
> (3.4)

This question is the crux of the incident, since it goes to the very heart of the meaning of the Sabbath day. Jesus wanted to know whether doing good (removing suffering) or being concerned with human rules and regulations were at the heart of what God

The people in the synagogue in Capernaum were amazed by the actions of Jesus. He was prepared to break any human law if human health and happiness was at stake.

intended for the Sabbath day. It was, of course, an impossible question for his opponents to answer. If they had answered that it was always good to help others, then Jesus would have asked them why they opposed what he was about to do. He was, after all, going to heal the man. On the other hand, those watching carefully could not be seen to be opposed to Jesus helping someone in need and taking away their suffering.

There was no reply from them. Mark tells us that Jesus was very sad because of the stubborn nature of his opponents. They were simply in the wrong, and it is never easy to admit that. Jesus told the man to stretch out his hand, and it was immediately healed (3.5).

The consequences

The Jewish law allowed anyone to save a person's life on the Sabbath if that life was under threat. However, clearly the life of this man was not in danger and he could easily have been cured on the following day. If that had happened the holiness of the Sabbath day would not have been disturbed. By insisting that the man was cured here and now Jesus was suggesting that there was little value in keeping the regulations of the holy day, and that was bound to upset his opponents. It seems that Jesus deliberately pushed the religious leaders into a tight corner in which they were forced to react – and their reaction was one that had the most serious repercussions for Jesus.

The healing of this man on the Sabbath day was the moment when two very unlikely allies, the Pharisees and the Herodians, decided to get rid of Jesus and made plans to kill him. The Pharisees were a religious group who wanted to keep the Jewish faith pure, while the Herodians were dedicated to keeping a descendant of Herod the Great on the throne of Judea. The Herodians are only mentioned in Mark's Gospel. Together with the other religious groups they were to prove successful in engineering the death of Jesus.

Mark wants us to know that these groups began making their murderous plans at a very early point in the ministry of Jesus. It was to be some time, however, before they would have the opportunity to put their plans into operation.

Key Points

1 When Jesus healed a man with a withered arm on the Sabbath day his opponents seized on the incident.
2 Jesus wondered aloud whether it was better to do good or to keep the law on the Sabbath day.
3 By healing the man Jesus suggested that the restrictions placed on the Sabbath day were of little value. This greatly upset the religious leaders.
4 The Pharisees and the Herodians, who were natural enemies, began to work together against Jesus even from this early point.

Work to do

1 a Describe, in your own words, the incident in which Jesus healed a man with a withered arm on the Sabbath day.
  b Why do you think that this story demonstrates the courage of Jesus?
  c Jesus put two options to the religious leaders, but there was a third option. What was that? Why do you think that Jesus did not consider it?
2 Why do you think that Jesus went ahead and healed the man with the withered arm on the Sabbath day, when he could have left it to the following day?
3 Describe briefly an incident when Jesus was criticised for healing a person. What exactly had Jesus said or done that led to the criticism?
4 Why do you think that the miracle of Jesus healing the man with the withered arm was remembered by the early Church and recorded by Mark in his Gospel?
5 Jesus cured many people who were sick and ill. What do you think that Christians today might learn from this?

In the Glossary

Gospel • Pharisees • Sabbath day • Scribe • Synagogue

7.5 Resurrection day

**Key
Question**

Why did the early Christians change from the Sabbath day to Sunday as their holy day?

Since most of the early Christians were Jews, it was natural for them to continue worshipping in the local synagogue on the Sabbath day, the Jewish holy day. They did this for some time after Jesus left the earth. Before long, however, Sunday – the day on which Jesus rose from the dead – replaced the Sabbath day as the time when Christians preferred to worship God. By moving the celebration of the Lord's Supper (Holy Communion) to a Sunday morning the Christians severed their last link with the Jewish faith.

The Lord's Day

Sunday became the Lord's Day. The word for Sunday in the Russian Orthodox Church is 'Voskresenye' (Resurrection). The name 'Sunday', however, was not given to the day until the time of Constantine, the first Christian Roman emperor, in the 4th century. He decreed that all non-essential work should stop on the Lord's Day, although agricultural work was allowed to continue. The name Sunday was applied to the day although it had been linked directly in the Roman Empire to the pagan worship of Sol, the sun-god, since well before the birth of Jesus.

When Christians made Sunday their special day, they were remembering three events:

1 Easter Sunday, the day on which Jesus rose from the dead. This belief, at the centre of the Christian faith, gave the day its joyful character. Christians were told that there was to be no kneeling or fasting on this day since it would destroy the happiness of the day. It was to be a day of celebration.

2 The first day of creation. Just as the Jews connected the Sabbath with the seventh day in the creation story when God rested from his creative work, so Christians connected Sunday with the first day of creation.

3 The coming of the Holy Spirit on the day of Pentecost. Christians today still celebrate this event – recorded in the Acts of the Apostles – in their festival of Whitsun or Pentecost, and look upon the events of that day as marking the birth of the Church.

A day of recreation

The nature and character of Sunday, and the way in which it is celebrated, varies from place to place. In those countries, such as Spain, where the Roman Catholic Church has predominated for centuries, church-going has usually been encouraged on Saturday evenings and Sunday mornings. The recent Catechism of the Catholic Church, published in 1994, placed all Catholics under a strong obligation to attend Mass in church on one of these days, but allowed the rest of Sunday to be used as a day of recreation (leisure). It did, however, point out that no one's leisure activity should involve someone else in work that they did not want to do.

Countries dominated by Protestantism have tried to restrict activities on a Sunday in the past, but this has now largely been abandoned. In 1994, for instance, the law was changed in Britain so that shops could open on a Sunday, although most of them are only permitted to open for a maximum of six hours. This change in the law was

Fewer and fewer people are going to church regularly on a Sunday – even some Christians prefer not to worship in a church on this day.

Sunday shopping – some people maintain that what has happened to Sundays is inevitable. Others believe that we have lost something very valuable in giving up one 'day of rest' out of seven.

surprisingly controversial. Opposition to it came from an alliance of those who wanted Sunday to remain special (Keep Sunday Special Campaign) and those who represented shop workers. A further bill allowed betting on a Sunday, making it possible for horse-racing to take place on this day. In the opinion of most people there is now little difference in Britain between Sunday and the other six days of the week.

Key Points

1 The early Christians observed the Sabbath day as their holy day.
2 By the 4th century, Sunday, the day of Christ's resurrection, had replaced the Sabbath day as the normal day for Christian worship. Christians also celebrate the first day of creation and the giving of the Holy Spirit at Pentecost on this day.
3 The character of Sundays in Britain changed considerably towards the end of the 20th century.

In the Glossary

Holy Communion • Holy Spirit • Lord's Supper • Mass • Pentecost • Protestant • Roman Catholic Church • Orthodox Church • Sabbath day • Sunday • Synagogue

Work to do

1 Brainstorming is a way of collecting contributions on a subject from everyone in a group. Appoint one member of your class to be the recorder and to keep the time. Block everything out of your mind for five minutes and ask each person to call out the things that come into their mind when they think of Sunday. The recorder must write each item down. Then make a list in your folder under two headings:
a Negative things about Sunday.
b Positive things about Sunday.
Now write, in about 500 words, what you think Sunday should be like. Try to be as positive as possible.
2 a The word 'Sunday' is much older than the Christian religion, going back to an ancient day dedicated to Sol, the Roman sun-god. This was celebrated on the first day of the week. Why do you think that Christians were content to take over a day that had pagan origins?
b Are you happy about the recent changes in the law concerning Sunday? Does it matter that all days of the week are now virtually identical?

Read

Mark
14.12–31

Key Question

What was said and done at the last meal that Jesus shared with his disciples?

We have seen how Jesus arrived in Jerusalem at the start of the last week of his life (see Unit 2.13). The people welcomed him as their promised Messiah (king) by throwing palm leaves and cloaks on the road in front of him. Three days later, on the eve of the start of the Jewish festival of Passover, Jesus met with his disciples to share the meal that started this time of celebration. By Jewish law this meal had to be eaten within the city limits of Jerusalem, and this is why Jesus had spent a long time travelling towards the city.

Two warnings and a promise

The account that Mark gives of this meal is set between two further examples of the weakness of his disciples. Jesus issued two warnings to his disciples.

He warned, first, that one of them would hand him over to the religious authorities and betray him (14.17–21). Mark does not identify Judas Iscariot as the culprit, although Matthew does. In Mark, Jesus simply says that Jesus will die as the Scriptures prophesied, but the outcome for the one who betrayed him would be terrible:

> "It would have been better for that man if he had never been born!"
> (14.21)

The second warning was that all of them would soon desert him and leave him friendless at his time of greatest need (14.27–31). This was so that a prophecy from the Jewish Scriptures could be fulfilled:

> "All of you will run away and leave me, for the scripture says, 'God will kill the shepherd and the sheep will all be scattered.'"
> (14.27)

Jesus immediately followed this up with the promise that, after he had been brought back to life, he would go ahead of his disciples to Galilee. The disciples, though, showed no indication of understanding what he was saying. Peter protested that he would remain faithful to Jesus – even if everyone else betrayed him. Jesus told him that he would disown Jesus three times before the cock crowed twice that very night.

The last meal

Mark's description of the last Passover meal that Jesus shared with his disciples is very simple. During the meal he took the loaf of bread, broke it, gave thanks and distributed it to his disciples. This was exactly what he had done when he fed a large crowd on just five loaves and two fish (see Unit 2.8). The symbolic significance of food is very much a part of the Passover ritual, and so his disciples would not have been surprised by the actions of Jesus. However, they would have been startled when he linked the bread and wine with his own death. He told them

Jesus used very familiar objects, like wine, bread and a grain of wheat, to teach his disciples about his coming death.

that the bread represented his own body which was shortly to be broken for them, and the whole world, on the cross.

Wine, diluted with water, was the common drink at all Jewish meals. As at all meals, God was thanked for the fruit of the vine. Again, though, Jesus went further and told his disciples that the wine in the goblet stood for his blood, which was going to be poured out on the cross for many people. His disciples, who were very familiar with the Jewish Scriptures, would have recognised the figure of the Suffering Servant of which Isaiah (chapter 53) spoke. Jesus was telling them that he was the Messiah – but a Messiah who would suffer and die for the sins of others.

No festival was as important in Judaism as the Passover. It looked back to the great deliverance of the Jews from slavery under Moses, and forward to the time when God would send his Messiah to set up his kingdom on earth. The Last Supper looked forward to the events that were about to unfold with the death of Jesus, and beyond that to the great banquet that would mark the end of time – when Jesus returned to the earth to set up God's kingdom. That is why Jesus told his disciples that he would not drink any wine again 'until the day I drink the new wine in the Kingdom of God' (14.25).

This is a seder plate. It holds some important symbolic foods during the Passover meal. These are used to teach young and old about the meaning of the festival.

Key Points

1 At the Last Supper Jesus warned his disciples that one of them would betray him and that all of them would soon desert him.
2 Jesus used the bread and wine at his last meal to teach his disciples about his forthcoming death.
3 These two symbols are at the heart of the service of Holy Communion – the most important service of worship in most Churches.

Work to do

1 Describe what happened during the Last Supper as it is recorded in Mark's Gospel. You should include:
   a the warnings of Jesus to his disciples;
   b the actions and words of Jesus.
2 What did Jesus say at the Last Supper as he took:
   a the bread;
   b the wine?
3 At the Last Supper, Jesus warned his disciples that one of them would betray him.
   a What did Jesus say about the person who would do this?
   b Why do you think that Judas betrayed Jesus?

In the Glossary

Disciple • Jerusalem • Judas Iscariot • Kingdom of God • Mark • Matthew • Messiah • Moses • Passover • Peter

8.2 The service of Holy Communion

Key Question

What is Holy Communion and what part does it play in Christian worship today?

The service of Holy Communion stands at the heart of worship in almost all Christian Churches. The clear link of the service with the life and death of Jesus makes it unique, and very special, amongst all acts of Christian worship. Through the roots of the service in the New Testament it is able to bring Christians into contact with the founder of their faith, Jesus of Nazareth. No other service is able to do this in quite the same way. Most Churches celebrate Holy Communion at least weekly, although in the Roman Catholic Church (where Holy Communion is called Mass) it is celebrated each day.

Back to the beginning

From the birth of the early Church, Christians used to meet together regularly to 'break bread'. They did this because they were convinced that Jesus had told them to do so – a belief that was underlined by the fact that all four Gospels and one of the epistles – 1 Corinthians – had reported the words of Jesus on which the service was based.

These accounts tell us that, on the night on which he was betrayed by Judas Iscariot, Jesus took a loaf of bread, blessed and broke it, and gave a piece to each of his disciples with the words:

> "Take it … this is my body."
> (14.22)

Moments later he took a goblet of wine and passed it around amongst his friends, saying to them:

> "This is my blood which is poured out for many, my blood which seals God's covenant."
> (14.24)

These words form the backbone of the modern service of Holy Communion. It is 'Holy' Communion since, in a unique way, the service brings together the divine (God) and the human (the worshipper).

Different names – different meanings

Ever since the meal was instituted by Jesus, Christians have disagreed amongst themselves over its precise meaning. These disagreements are reflected, to some extent, in the different names given to the service by the various Churches:

a In the Roman Catholic Church it is called the Mass, from the final words of the old Latin service, *Ite missa est* ('Go, it is ended').

By breaking bread and drinking wine with his disciples Jesus was giving them, and all Christians, two symbols by which to remember his death for all time.

b In the Anglican Church it is known mainly as the Eucharist ('thanksgiving'), although some prefer to call it Holy Communion. Some Anglicans who are close to the Roman Catholic Church in their way of worshipping call it the Mass.

c In Orthodox Churches the service is called the Holy Liturgy – a divine service of worship which follows a traditional order of service (the liturgy).

d In Free Churches, such as the Baptists and Methodists, it is either the Breaking of Bread or the Lord's Supper. Both of these titles come from the New Testament.

Only the Quakers and the Salvation Army, amongst the main Christian Churches, do not celebrate Holy Communion – or any of the other sacraments.

Roman Catholic and Orthodox Churches understand the service of Holy Communion in a very different way to Protestant Churches:

a The Roman Catholic and Orthodox Churches teach that Christ is actually present in the bread and wine once they have been consecrated by the priest. The bread and wine become the body and blood of Christ (a belief called 'transubstantiation') and the service becomes a sacrificial re-enactment of the death of Jesus on the cross.

b The Protestant Churches, including Anglicans and the Free Churches, believe that Holy Communion is a service of remembrance through which worshippers can arrive at a deeper understanding and appreciation of the love of Jesus. The bread and wine are only symbols to help this, and nothing happens to them during the service.

In the Anglican Church Holy Communion is often called the Eucharist, a word which means 'thanksgiving'. Giving thanks to God for the death of Jesus lies at the heart of the service of the Eucharist.

Work to do

1 Some Christians celebrate Holy Communion sitting together around a table. Why do you think they prefer to do this?

2 a What did Jesus say as he shared bread and wine with his disciples?

b How do Christians disagree in their views of the meaning of the words of Jesus as he broke the bread and shared the wine?

Key Points

1 Holy Communion is the most important service in most Churches.

2 The early Christians met regularly to 'break bread' because Jesus had told them to do so.

3 There are many different names for the service of Holy Communion among the various Churches.

4 Roman Catholic and Orthodox churches believe in transubstantiation but Protestant Churches do not.

5 The Quakers and the Salvation Army do not celebrate Holy Communion.

In the Glossary

Anglican Church • Baptist Church • Breaking of Bread • Church of England • Epistle • Eucharist • Free Churches • Gospel • Holy Communion • Holy Liturgy • Liturgy • Lord's Supper • Mass • Methodist Church • New Testament • Orthodox Church • Priest • Protestant • Quakers • Roman Catholic Church • Sacrament • Salvation Army • Transubstantiation

8.3 The Eucharist

Which Christians celebrate the Eucharist, and what does the service mean to them?

In the Anglican Church, the service of Holy Communion is often called the Eucharist ('thanksgiving'). It stands at the centre of worship in most churches. In their worship some churches still use the old Prayer Book, the Book of Common Prayer published in 1662, which emphasises:

a the sufferings of Jesus that led up to his death on the cross;

b the humble and penitent approach of the worshipper to God as he or she comes forward to receive the sacrament of the Eucharist from the priest. The confession of a person's sins at the start of the service is a very important part of the Eucharist.

A family meal

The Anglican Church introduced another Prayer Book in 1980 (the *Alternative Service Book* or ASB), which was written in more modern language. In the ASB, which most Anglican Churches use, the Eucharist is much more of a family meal in which everyone is able to freely share as equal members of the Anglican community. Some churches require that each participant has been baptised and confirmed in the Anglican Church, although this is not always the case.

The idea of the Eucharist as a family meal is stressed by the giving of the 'Peace' just before the bread and wine are distributed among the worshippers. At this moment in the service the people shake hands, hug or kiss while saying the words:

"The Peace of the Lord be with you."

As with all Communion services, the giving and receiving of the bread and wine is the most important part of the worship. Once the priest has blessed the bread and wine in front of the people, he says to all of the communicants (those taking Communion):

"Draw near and receive the body of our Lord Jesus Christ, which was given for you, and his blood, which was shed for you. Take this in remembrance that Christ died for you, and feed on him in your hearts by faith with thanksgiving."

As he gives the bread, the priest says to each person:

"The body of Christ."

And as he hands them the wine he says:

"The blood of Christ."

They reply each time:

"Amen [so be it]."

Reflecting on the death of Jesus is a very important part of the Eucharist.

Celebrating the Eucharist

The frequency with which the Eucharist is celebrated is a guide to the importance which a particular church attaches to the service. In Anglo-Catholic Anglican churches the Eucharist is celebrated several times a week, if not daily. In most Anglican churches, however, the Eucharist is usually celebrated once each Sunday and once more during the week. In addition, it is celebrated on special church festivals such as Easter Day and Ascension Day.

For Anglo-Catholics the Eucharist is understood as if it was the Roman Catholic Mass (see Unit 8.4). During the service it is believed that the bread and wine become the actual body and blood of Jesus. Low Church (Evangelical) Anglicans, however, share the general Protestant belief that the Eucharist is a commemoration of the Last Supper. For both groups, however, the service is one in which God blesses them in a way that does not happen in any other service.

In the time of Jesus wine was a very common drink in Palestine. It is important that the sacraments make use of the familiar and give it a real spiritual significance.

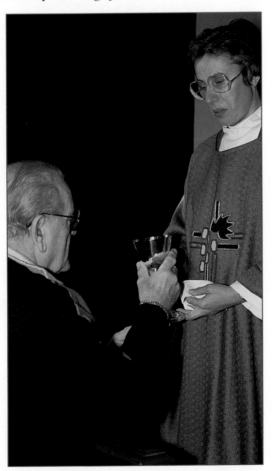

(see Unit 8.4)

For your Information

This prayer is prayed by the priest during the Eucharist:

"... Who in the same night that he was betrayed, took bread and gave you thanks; he broke it and gave it to his disciples, saying: 'Take, eat; this is my body which is given for you, do this in remembrance of me.' In the same way, after supper, he took the cup and gave thanks; he gave it to them, saying: 'Drink this, all of you; this is the blood of my new covenant, which is shed for you, and for many, for the forgiveness of sin. Do this, as often as you drink it, in remembrance of me.'"

Key Points

1 The Eucharist is the most important service in Anglican churches.
2 The modern Eucharist service is a family meal shared between all members of the church family. The giving of the Peace underlines this.
3 Some Anglican churches celebrate the Eucharist many times a week, although weekly or twice weekly is more common.
4 Some Anglicans have a Roman Catholic understanding of the Eucharist's meaning, while others adopt a Protestant approach.

Work to do

Answer each of these questions about the Anglican Eucharist service in your own words:
1 What is the Eucharist, and what does the word mean?
2 Which two Prayer Books are used in Anglican Churches, and how do they emphasise different things in the Eucharist service?
3 What are the two qualifications needed by anyone who wishes to participate in the Anglican Eucharist?
4 What do you think they mean when many Anglican churches call the Eucharist a family or a community meal?

In the Glossary

Anglican Church • Eucharist • Holy Communion • Mass • Priest • Roman Catholic Church • Sacrament

8.4 The Mass

Key Question

What is distinctive about the Roman Catholic service of Mass, and why is it important?

Roman Catholics share the word 'Eucharist' with Anglicans. This comes from the Greek word for 'thanksgiving', and draws attention to the fact that believers give thanks for the blessings that they share through this sacrament. In the Roman Catholic Church, however, the term 'Mass' is more likely to be used. The actual origin of this word is obscure, but it probably comes from the very last words of the old Latin Mass, *Ite missa est* ('Go, it is ended').

For most Roman Catholics, going to Mass and receiving the bread and wine are at the centre of their lives as Christians. The Mass is celebrated daily in every Catholic church, and practising Catholics are obliged to attend the service regularly. The service is a renewal of their faith as they listen to the Bible readings, pray together and take the consecrated bread (called the 'host') and the wine.

What happens during Mass

Catholics believe that to take part in the Mass they must be cleansed from their sins. A Catholic who has committed a serious sin can receive absolution (forgiveness) through confession to a priest. Everyone, though, who is present at the Mass receives forgiveness for lesser (venial) sins through the 'penitential rite' at the start of the service. All Catholics make the 'sign of the cross' with holy water as they enter church as a way of preparing themselves for the service. The holy water is found in a stoup (container) just inside the door of the church.

The Mass is divided into two parts:

1 The Liturgy of the Word. As the Mass opens, the people are invited to repent for their sins and seek God's forgiveness. The priest pronounces this forgiveness. Three passages from the Bible – from the Old Testament, the Gospels and the Epistles – are read before the priest gives his sermon (homily). The people then say the Nicene Creed together.

2 The Liturgy of the Eucharist. The gifts of money, bread and wine are brought forward to the altar. The priest consecrates them to God. It is at this point that the bread and wine become the actual body and blood of Jesus. This is called 'transubstantiation', and a bell is rung to indicate that it has happened. The belief in transubstantiation is the main difference between the Roman Catholic and the Protestant service of Eucharist.

The people join together in the Lord's Prayer (the 'Our Father') to pray for their daily food and forgiveness. Before sharing the bread and wine they give each other the sign of peace as an open demonstration of their love for one another – and for God. The priest then takes Holy Communion before distributing it amongst the people. In larger churches the distribution is often carried out by servers.

A worshipper entering a Catholic church dips their fingers into holy water and makes the sign of the cross on their body.

The thin, round wafer consecrated by the priest during Mass is called the 'host'; it is believed to be the body of Jesus.

Finally, everyone is sent out into the world to help their neighbour, especially if that person is in need. By serving others they are not only helping those in need but serving God as well. They are also strengthening their own spiritual lives, something they have already done by sharing in the Mass together. The priest dismisses members of the congregation with the words:

"Go in peace to love and serve the Lord."

Key Points

1 The service of Holy Communion in a Roman Catholic church is called the Mass.
2 The Mass is celebrated each day in a Catholic church. The service is at the centre of the life of each Roman Catholic. The first part of the service centres around the forgiveness of sins and the reading of the Bible.
3 In the celebration of the Eucharist the host and wine become the body and blood of Jesus. This belief is called transubstantiation. Catholics believe in transubstantiation and Protestants do not.

For your Information

The Catechism of the Catholic Church says:

"In the Eucharist Christ gives us the very body which he gave up for us on the cross, the very blood which he 'poured out for many for the forgiveness of sins'. The Mass is so important for all Catholics because it is the means by which their spiritual lives are renewed day by day. Not only does the Mass unite Catholics with Jesus Christ but it also unites them with each other."

Work to do

1 The sermon or homily given by the priest during the Mass is described as 'the breaking of the bread of the Word'. Try to explain what you think this phrase might mean.
2 St Paul wrote:

"Because there is the one loaf of bread, all of us, though many, are one body, for we all share the same loaf."
(1 Corinthians 10.17)

a What point do you think Paul is making about the symbolic importance of the Mass or Eucharist here?
b How does the Peace of the Mass underline the importance that everyone is the same in this sacrament?
c How does the Mass underline the belief that all Christians should work together for peace and justice in the world?

In the Glossary

Altar • Bible • Epistle • Eucharist • Gospel • Holy Communion • Liturgy • Mass • Old Testament • Priest • Protestant • Roman Catholic Church • Transubstantiation

8.5 The Holy Liturgy

Key Question

What is the Holy Liturgy, and what part does it play in the worship of the Orthodox Church?

The liturgy ('the people's work of thanksgiving') is any service, in any church, that follows a form laid down, and made holy, by a long tradition of use and worship. In the Orthodox Church the term is applied, in particular, to the Holy or Divine Liturgy – the service of Holy Communion. This service has the same form today as it had in the 5th century, following a liturgy associated with St John Chrysostom. Like the Mass, the Holy Liturgy falls into two clear parts, the Liturgy of the Word and the Liturgy of the Faithful.

The Liturgy of the Word

The first part of the service includes prayers, Bible readings and a sermon. The climax comes when the priest, carrying the Book of the Gospels high above his head, comes through the Royal Doors in the middle of the iconostasis (see photograph). The iconostasis is the screen in front of the High Altar (Holy Table) which is covered with icons (holy paintings). As the Gospels pass, the people sing:

> "Holy God, holy and mighty, holy and immortal, have mercy on us."

Surrounded by attendants carrying candles, the priest reads a passage from the Gospels before returning through the iconostasis to the High Altar.

The Liturgy of the Faithful

Most of the Liturgy of the Faithful is conducted behind the iconostasis, although the people can see and hear enough of what is going on to follow the service. The iconostasis has an important symbolic part to play in the Holy Liturgy. It symbolises the gulf that exists between God and human beings because of their sin. This gulf is so great that only the priest, ordained to God, can enter God's presence. The people can only glimpse the presence of God from a distance.

There are three parts to the Liturgy of the Faithful.

1 It begins with the preparation of the bread and wine for Communion. The priest stands at the altar and the Royal Doors are closed. The bread and wine are laid on the High Altar. This shows the holiness of the death of Jesus and the symbols of bread and wine by which it is represented.

The iconostasis, covered with icons, stands between the altar and the people in an Orthodox church.

Finally the priest raises the bread high and breaks it – a part of the service called the 'elevation' – while the choir sings and bells are rung.

2 After the bread and wine have been blessed and consecrated to God, the priest brings them through the Royal Doors and the people stand, or kneel, at the front of the church to receive them. The bread, dipped in wine, is placed at the back of the mouth on a silver spoon.

3 After taking Communion everyone comes up to kiss the cross that the priest is holding. A small piece of bread is shared together as a sign of fellowship and love – just as the early Christians shared their meals together.

The beauty of the Holy Liturgy

Each way of celebrating Holy Communion in the different Churches emphasises something different. The beauty of the Holy Liturgy is a very important part of its meaning. Orthodox Christians believe that they are celebrating an 'eternal liturgy' since everything on earth is a pattern of a heavenly image. Through experiencing the liturgy they are able to imagine what it is going to be like in heaven – and enjoy a very limited experience of it. In particular, through the Holy Liturgy they can gain a glimpse of the members of the Trinity – God the Father, God the Son and God the Holy Spirit. Taking part in the Holy Liturgy is like the corner of a curtain covering heaven being drawn aside, just for a moment.

Key Points

1 The service of Holy Liturgy in the Orthodox Church has remained unchanged for centuries. The first part of the service, the Liturgy of the Word, ends with the priest reading a passage from the Gospels.
2 The second part of the service, the Liturgy of the Faithful, consists of Communion. The bread and wine are brought through the Royal Doors, and are given together on a silver spoon.
3 The beauty of the service is an important part of its meaning. The service is based on the original heavenly liturgy, and gives a glimpse of heaven.

The priest prepares the bread and wine for use in the Holy Liturgy on the altar and out of sight of the people.

Work to do

1 Why do you think that in the Orthodox Church, like the Catholic Church, the priest takes the bread and wine before it is offered to the people?
2 What do you think is the symbolic importance of the bread being dipped in wine instead of the two elements being offered separately – as they are in the other Christian Churches?
3 Do you see any symbolic importance in the practice of placing the bread on a silver spoon, and putting it directly into the mouths of worshippers?
4 Why do you think that Orthodox worshippers see the Holy Liturgy as being a foretaste of heaven – and what do you think they mean by this?

In the Glossary

Altar • Bible • Gospel • Holy Communion • Holy Liturgy • Holy Spirit • Icon • Iconostasis • Liturgy • Mass • Orthodox Church • Priest • Royal Doors • Sermon • Trinity

8.6 The Lord's Supper (the Breaking of Bread)

Key Question

What is distinctive about the way that the Lord's Supper is celebrated in Free Churches?

Free Churches, such as the Baptists and Methodists, have two favourite terms for Holy Communion, the service in which they remember and draw strength from the death and resurrection of Jesus. Both of the terms are taken directly from the New Testament:

a **The Breaking of Bread** – taken from Acts 20.7. The early Christians often came together to share an ordinary meal with each other at which bread was 'broken'.

b **The Lord's Supper** – an expression used by Paul in 1 Corinthians 11.20.

What happens in the Lord's Supper

Protestants try to keep their worship as close to the Bible as possible. The story in Mark, and the other Gospels, of the Last Supper provides the pattern for them to follow when they celebrate the Lord's Supper. This celebration falls into four distinct parts.

1 The people confess their sins to God before listening to a passage from the New Testament. This passage will either describe the last meal of Jesus with his disciples (Mark 14.12–31) or Paul's description of the meal (1 Corinthians 11.17–34). A short time is spent by the minister explaining the passage, and a collection for the poor of the church is often taken up. This is a practice copied by many churches from the early Church.

2 The bread and wine are either placed on the Communion table (there is no altar in Free Churches) or a cloth covering them is removed. The wine is in small individual glasses, while the bread is cut up in small squares. The bread and wine are consecrated to God as the minister reads the words of Jesus at the Last Supper.

3 The people remain seated while a loaf of bread, or small pieces, is passed around to them in their seats. As each person takes the bread so they eat it at once. This symbolises the Protestant belief that each person must respond to God for themselves as individuals needing his help and grace.

In the Baptist Church the bread and the wine are brought to worshippers by the leaders of the church.

4 The wine is given to the people in slotted trays by the deacons or elders of the church. The people wait until the wine has been served to everyone before they drink together as a mark 'of our oneness in Christ'. This, too, has a symbolic meaning. The act of drinking together underlines Protestant belief that church fellowship is extremely important. The empty glasses are placed in special slots in the back of the seats in front. They are collected up after the service has finished.

The meaning of the Lord's Supper

Unlike Roman Catholic and Orthodox Christians, Protestants do not believe that anything happens to the wine and bread during the service. The Catholic belief in transubstantiation (that the bread and wine become the body and blood of Christ) was emphatically rejected by Protestants in Europe during the Reformation in the 16th century.

The bread and wine simply act as symbols of the death of Jesus, and so lead the worshipper into a deeper understanding of that event. As they are taken, and consumed, they act as a stimulus to meditation and reflection. This is why the minister tells the congregation before distributing the bread and wine:

> "Feed on him [Christ] in your hearts by faith."

Key Points

1 In the Free Churches the service of Holy Communion can be called the Breaking of Bread or the Lord's Supper.
2 The Breaking of Bread service uses individual pieces of bread and wine glasses. Protestant religion has always been highly individualistic.
3 The bread and wine only have symbolic importance. The importance of the service lies in the worshippers' ability to reflect deeply on the death of Jesus – and to remember it.

Work to do

1 Read Mark 14.22–24. Make a list in your folder of as many ways as possible in which the Protestant service of the Breaking of Bread resembles the last meal that Jesus shared with his disciples.
2 Read 1 Corinthians 11.23–26 in which Paul claims to have had a revelation from God about the Lord's Supper. Answer these questions in your own words:
   a Is there any support in this passage for the Free Church title of 'Breaking of Bread' for the service of Holy Communion?
   b What did Jesus say to his disciples as he handed the bread and wine to them?
   c What support does there seem to be for the Free Church belief that the Lord's Supper should essentially be a time for remembering, and reflecting on, the death of Jesus?
   d What are the believers in a Free Church doing when they eat the bread and drink the wine?

In the Breaking of Bread service the bread and wine are simply symbols prompting people to reflect deeply on the death and resurrection of Jesus.

In the Glossary

Altar • Baptist Church • Bible • Breaking of Bread • Communion table • Disciple • Free Churches • Gospel • Holy Communion • Last Supper • Lord's Supper • Mark • Methodist Church • New Testament • Orthodox Church • Paul • Protestant • Reformation • Roman Catholic Church • Transubstantiation

Key Question

What is baptism and what does it symbolise?

The sacraments form a very important part of worship in most churches. These are services or ceremonies which can be directly traced back to the New Testament or to the worship of the early Church. Christians believe that these sacraments are special channels for bringing God's blessing to them. To do this, the sacraments make use of familiar, everyday ingredients such as bread, wine, water and oil.

In the Roman Catholic and Orthodox Churches there are seven sacraments, although the Orthodox Church prefers to call them 'mysteries'. They are:
- Holy Communion, also called the Mass (Roman Catholic Church) or the Holy Liturgy (Orthodox Church)
- infant baptism
- confirmation
- penance
- ordination to the priesthood
- holy unction (anointing the sick with oil)
- marriage.

The sacraments use common objects, such as bread and wine, to convey important spiritual truths.

In most Protestant churches there are just two sacraments – Holy Communion and baptism. Some of the other sacraments do take place, such as ordination and marriage, but they are regarded as services rather than sacraments. Only the Salvation Army and the Quakers, of the main churches, do not celebrate any of the sacraments.

In Unit 8 we looked at the most important of these sacraments – Holy Communion. Here we look at the sacrament of baptism.

Baptism

Baptism is the service by which people become members of the Church. There are frequent references to it in the Acts of the Apostles and the letters (epistles) of Paul, and Jesus was baptised by John the Baptist (see Unit 9.3) in the River Jordan. In the early Christian Church, in the period covered by the New Testament, only adults were baptised, but later on Christian parents wanted their children baptised to share in the blessings of Church membership as well. Gradually infant, rather than adult, baptism became normal in almost all of the churches.

In the 17th century, however, a small group of people left the Church of England because they believed that only adults, who had their own faith in Christ, should be baptised. They were first known as Anabaptists (those who were 'baptised again'), but soon the Baptist Church was born. This Church, now one of the largest in the world, still insists on believer's baptism (see Unit 9.5) before a person can be received into church membership. Children are 'dedicated to God' in a special service, but they are not baptised.

Why be baptised?

Whether babies or adults are baptised, most Christians agree on the symbolism behind the service. They point out that:
- a person must repent from their sins and turn to Jesus as their Saviour before baptism can have any real meaning. The person who treads this path is promised God's forgiveness. In the case of a baby, the promise to repent has to be made by parents and godparents on the child's behalf. The child is then able to return to church, many years later, and make the same promise for themselves in the confirmation service;
- the water used to baptise a person symbolises their cleansing from sin and the rebirth that they receive from God;
- the person being baptised shares in the death and resurrection of Jesus. This symbolism is brought out very strongly in believer's baptism;

● baptism brings people together and unites them, as the baptised person becomes a member of the Christian Church. This person begins to share in the life of God which continues beyond death into eternity.

Key Points

1 The sacraments are an important element of worship for many Christians. The Roman Catholic and Orthodox Churches recognise seven sacraments – the Anglicans two.

2 Baptism is one of only two sacraments which can be traced directly back to the ministry of Jesus.

3 Only adults are baptised in the Baptist Church. Most of the other Churches baptise children.

4 Repentance from sin must come before baptism. Cleansing follows through the waters of baptism. The baptised person shares in the death and resurrection of Jesus when they are baptised.

Work to do

1 St Augustine was a Christian leader from the 5th century. He defined a sacrament as 'the visible form of an invisible grace'.
   a What is a sacrament?
   b Name three material elements which are used in different sacraments.
   c What form did the sacrament of baptism take in the early Church and how did that change?
   d St Augustine made an important point about each sacrament. What is that?
   e What is the attitude of the Salvation Army and the Quakers towards the sacraments? Can you find out why?

2 Whilst most Churches call these special services 'sacraments', the Orthodox Church prefers to call them 'mysteries'. This difference highlights a very important truth about the sacraments. What do you think this is?

3 Find out about each of the following and explain their meaning in a paragraph:
   a confirmation;
   b penance;
   c ordination to the priesthood;
   d holy unction.

4 List four things that most Christians agree on about baptism.

Running water has always been an important Christian symbol for cleansing and life-giving.

In the Glossary

Baptism • Baptist Church • Believer's baptism • Church of England • Confirmation • Epistle • Holy Communion • Holy Liturgy • Holy Unction • Infant baptism • John the Baptist • Mass • New Testament • Ordination • Orthodox Church • Paul • Penance • Protestant • Quakers • Roman Catholic Church • Sacrament • Salvation Army

9.2 God's messenger

 Read

Mark 1.1–8

Key Question

What part did John the Baptist, his cousin, play in the life of Jesus?

John the Baptist was born about 7 BCE to an elderly couple, Zechariah, a priest, and his wife, Elizabeth. They had long given up hope of having a child and they looked upon Elizabeth's pregnancy as a miracle. The child grew up largely in the wilderness of Judea, and it was there that he was called by God to be a prophet.

By the time that John came out of obscurity and began to baptise people in the River Jordan the Jews had spent many years under Roman domination. There was still a great expectation in the Jewish community, though, that God would not allow this state of affairs to continue for much longer. The Jewish Scriptures had led the people to expect a deliverer (the Messiah), sent by God, who would throw all oppressors out of Israel for ever. The Messiah would then set up God's kingdom on earth.

Before the Messiah appeared, however, the Scriptures promised that a messenger would be sent to prepare the people for his coming. Jews were familiar with the idea of a messenger ('forerunner'), since every important religious leader was preceded in public by someone who announced their coming and prepared a way through the crowds for them. Mark used two quotations from the Old Testament – Malachi 3.1 and Isaiah 40.3–11 – to introduce John the Baptist as that promised messenger who was sent by God to prepare the people for the coming of their Messiah, Jesus.

John the Baptist

What Josephus, an important 1st-century Jewish historian, said about John the Baptist (see information box) supports what we know of him from Mark's Gospel. John's diet of locusts and wild honey, together with his coat of camel's hair tied around the middle with a leather belt (1.6), suggest that he followed the strict lifestyle of a desert monk. He was probably influenced by the Old Testament Nazarite vow, which demanded that a person abstained from alcohol, did not cut his hair and avoided all contact with dead bodies to show his commitment to God.

Mark provides us with two additional pieces of important information about John the Baptist:

1 Josephus mentions that John baptised people, and this fits in with Mark's description of him as 'John the baptiser' in 6.14. His appearance on the Palestinian scene must have created quite a stir, since 'many people from the province of Judea and the city of Jerusalem' went out to hear John. Many of them confessed their sins and were baptised by him beneath the waters of the River Jordan. Although baptism through total immersion in water was used by many Jewish religious groups at the time, John gave it a totally new meaning – and provided the foundation for its later adoption by the Christian Church. Both infant and believer's baptism owe a debt to the work of John.

This stained-glass window shows John the Baptist baptising Jesus in the River Jordan.

2 John looked forward to the coming of Jesus: he was the forerunner of Jesus. John knew that his importance lay only in his relationship with Jesus. He was sent to prepare the people for Jesus' coming, and he acknowledged that Jesus was much greater than he himself was. John said about Jesus:

> "The man who will come after me is much greater than I am. I am not good enough even to bend down and untie his sandals. I baptise you with water, but he will baptise you with the Holy Spirit."
> (1.7–8)

Many churches celebrate the season of Advent in December as a time of preparation for Christmas. It begins on the fourth Sunday before Christmas day at the end of November. During Advent, Christians not only prepare themselves for the coming of Jesus into the world but also think about the part that John the Baptist played in making this possible. They recognise that John played a very important, if brief, role in the life of Jesus of Nazareth.

For your Information

Josephus, the Jewish historian, said this about John the Baptist:

> "John encouraged the Jews to live righteous lives, to practise justice towards their fellows and holiness towards God, and so doing to join him in baptism. The baptism does not secure forgiveness unless the soul is already thoroughly cleansed by good behaviour."

Key Points

1 The birth of John the Baptist to his elderly parents was considered to be a miracle.
2 John was God's messenger sent to announce the arrival of Jesus – the Messiah. He called on the people to repent of their sins before he baptised them in the River Jordan.
3 John baptised the people by total immersion. This gave some parts of the Christian Church the symbol of believer's baptism. Most Christian Churches, however, continue to baptise infants.
4 The work of John is celebrated by many Christians in the season of Advent – the time of preparation for the coming of Jesus at Christmas.

Work to do

1 Mark begins his Gospel with an account of the teaching of John the Baptist.
   a What was John preparing the people for, and how did he do it?
   b What did John say about himself and the man who was to follow him?
   c In your opinion, why did Mark think that John the Baptist had an important part to play in the ministry of Jesus?
2 Answer each of these questions in your own words:
   a What did the prophets Malachi and Isaiah predict about John the Baptist?
   b What was John preparing the people for, and how did he do it?
   c What did John say about the man who was to come after him?
   d What did John tell the people to do – and what did he promise them if they did?
3 Describe two ways in which Mark thought that John the Baptist was important.
4 What do you think that John meant when he said about Jesus: 'I baptise you with water, but he will baptise you with the Holy Spirit' (1.8)?
5 What was the relationship between John the Baptist and Jesus? Refer to the opening verses of Mark's Gospel in your answer.
6 State two ways in which Mark thought that John the Baptist was important.

In the Glossary

Advent • Baptism • Gospel • Holy Spirit • Jerusalem • John the Baptist • Mark • Messiah • Old Testament • Prophet

9.3　The baptism and temptation of Jesus

 Read

Mark
1.9–13

 **Key Question**

What does Mark tell us about the baptism and temptation of Jesus, and why are these two events linked together?

Mark tells us that many people from the province of Judea and the city of Jerusalem went to listen to John the Baptist and were baptised by him. Then, out of total obscurity, Jesus arrived on the banks of the River Jordan and asked John the Baptist to baptise him. After baptising Jesus, John disappeared from the Gospel story, only reappearing when Mark describes, at some length, his death at the hands of Herod Antipas (6.14–29).

All of the Synoptic writers (Matthew, Mark and Luke) link the baptism of Jesus with his temptation in the wilderness (Matthew 3.13–4.11; Mark 1.9–13; Luke 3.21–4.13) which follows directly afterwards. In fact, there is good reason to see the one event, the baptism, as leading on inevitably to the other, the temptation.

The baptism of Jesus

The irony of Jesus, the sinless Son of God, coming to be baptised for the forgiveness of his sins struck both Matthew and Luke as unusual, but not Mark. For Mark, the heart of the baptism story is found in what happened immediately after the event. Mark, as usual, is in a breathless hurry, and provides us with just three pieces of information about the baptism of Jesus:

1 'As soon as Jesus came up out of the water, he saw heaven opening' (1.10). The Gospel writers, as all Jews at the time, believed that the sky was a great dome stretching over the earth with a number of kingdoms above it and God's kingdom the highest one of all. When he came up from the water, having been baptised, only Jesus saw the heavens split wide open, which suggests that, for Mark, this was an internal vision given to Jesus rather than an actual event.

2 'and the Spirit coming down on him like a dove' (1.10). Jews believed that the Holy Spirit had been active in the world, carrying out God's wishes, since its creation. The prophets of old, for instance, had been inspired to speak out by the Holy Spirit. Here the Spirit came down on Jesus 'like a dove' – a clear reference to the Old Testament story of Noah and the flood

In this modern stained-glass window the dove, representing the Holy Spirit, hovers above Jesus at his baptism.

(Genesis 6.9–9.17). Since this time the dove, a bird of peace, has been the most popular symbol of the Holy Spirit.

3 'And a voice came from heaven, "You are my own dear Son. I am pleased with you"' (1.11). These words, taken from Psalm 2.7 and Isaiah 42.1, underline the Christian belief that Jesus was God's Son.

The baptism of Jesus was an important event, although Mark, as we have seen, only mentioned it briefly. It showed the special relationship that Jesus had with God, his Father, and the Holy Spirit. At the baptism God, for the first time, acknowledged that Jesus was his Son. This acknowledgement was immediately going to be put to the test during the temptation that followed. The story of the baptism also provided the inspiration for the practice of baptism in the Church – especially the baptism of adult believers (see Unit 9.5).

The temptation of Jesus

Directly after Jesus' baptism Mark tells us that 'the Spirit made him go into the desert' (1.12). What followed is dealt with briefly by Mark, who underlines two important points about the event:

1 The conflict between Jesus and the powers of evil was inevitable as soon as the identity of Jesus became known – as it had done at his baptism. This conflict, between Jesus and Satan (the Prince of darkness), evil spirits and the religious authorities, is one of the most important themes in Mark's Gospel.

2 Jesus spent 40 days in the wilderness before the tempting began. The wilderness, the rocky hill-country between Jerusalem and Jericho, was believed to be the natural home of demons and evil spirits. Jews were very reluctant to travel through the area for this reason. Christians are divided over whether the temptation actually took place, or whether it was a series of 'inner battles' that took place in the mind of Jesus. Certainly many Christians suffering persecution at the time of Mark must have believed themselves to be in a life and death struggle with Satan himself – just as Jesus did. By looking to Jesus, as the strong Son of God, and by following his example,

Christians were taught to overcome temptation – whatever form it took. The story of the temptation was above all one offering comfort and encouragement to those who felt alone and lost when persecution came.

Key Points

1 The baptism of Jesus in the Synoptic Gospels is linked with his temptation by Satan in the wilderness.
2 The irony of the sinless Jesus being baptised by John was picked up by Matthew and Luke but not by Mark. For everyone else John's baptism was linked to a repentance for sins.
3 When he was baptised it was only Jesus who saw the heavens split open, which suggests that it was a personal vision. The Spirit descended on Jesus in a dove-like form.
4 The temptation tested Jesus' awareness of himself to be God's chosen Son.

Work to do

1 a Who baptised Jesus and how did he receive his name?
b What was the symbolism behind the Holy Spirit descending on Jesus 'like a dove'?
c What did the voice from heaven say to Jesus, and who did Mark believe the voice to be?
d What do you think the importance to Mark was of no one, except Jesus, hearing the voice?
2 Suggest two ways in which the baptism of Jesus by John the Baptist marked a turning-point in Jesus' life.
3 The baptism of Jesus as described by Mark in his Gospel has three elements. What are they? Make a one-sentence comment on each of them.
4 What do you think the temptation of Jesus in the desert was really about?

In the Glossary

Baptism • Herod Antipas • Holy Spirit • Jerusalem • John the Baptist • Luke • Mark • Matthew • Moses • Old Testament • Prophet • Satan • Synoptic Gospels • Torah

9.4   Infant baptism

Key Question

What is infant baptism, and why is it an important part of worship in many Churches?

As we saw in Unit 9.3, Jesus emerged from obscurity at the beginning of his ministry to be baptised by John the Baptist in the River Jordan. Jesus was 30 years old at the time – John only baptised adults. There is no clear reference at all in the New Testament to the baptism of babies or young children, and it was not until the 4th century that Christian families began to have their babies baptised. The belief had grown up by that time that unbaptised babies, many of whom died before reaching their first birthday, would not enter heaven. For this reason Christian parents placed a great deal of importance on having their young children baptised. They were terrified by the thought that their children might not reach heaven.

What is infant baptism?

Originally the word 'baptism' was applied to sheep who were dipped into water to kill any parasites on their bodies. The same idea was applied to people who were dipped beneath the water in baptism – the water cleansed them from their sins. Baptism was soon linked with Church membership, which was only open to those who had been baptised first. Three Churches are most strongly committed to the practice of infant baptism – the Roman Catholic, Orthodox and the Anglican Churches – although they do not totally agree on the meaning and significance of the service.

Orthodox Church

In the Orthodox Church baptism and confirmation follow each other in the same service, which is carried out when a baby is eight days old – the same day on which a Jewish male child is circumcised. The Orthodox service, called chrismation, begins with a prayer that the child may come to know God and all his commandments. The child's clothes are then removed to symbolise the leaving behind of the old life with its sinful habits. The service which follows falls into three parts:
- the priest blesses the baptismal water and breathes on it in the shape of a cross;

- a pre-baptism anointing of the child with the 'oil of gladness';
- the baptism itself.

In the baptism proper the baby is held up in the font facing east (a symbol of resurrection) and submerged beneath the water three times. The priest says to the child:

> "This servant of God is baptised in the name of the Father, Amen. And of the Son, Amen. And of the Holy Spirit, Amen."

The baby is then dressed in a new robe (the robe of righteousness), showing that he or she has become a new person, and anointed with oil (chrism) to demonstrate that the Holy Spirit has been received.

Roman Catholic and Anglican Churches

The Roman Catholic and Anglican services of infant baptism follow the same general pattern. The child is presented for baptism by parents and god-parents who promise to take responsibility for the child's spiritual welfare until he or she grows up. The child is baptised with water being poured over him or her from the font by the priest three times with the words:

> "I baptise you in the name of the Father, the Son and the Holy Spirit."

Thousands of couples still bring their babies to church to be baptised although they are not churchgoers themselves.

The priest makes the sign of the cross on the baby's forehead. After the baby has been baptised, a lighted candle is often handed to the parents to show that the child has moved from spiritual darkness to light. The whole congregation tells the child:

"We welcome you into the Lord's family. We are members together of Christ: we are children of the same Heavenly Father, we are inheritors together of the Kingdom of God."

As these words make clear, the Anglican and Roman Catholic Churches see themselves as spiritual families. Through being baptised a child is welcomed into the family. From now onwards the 'family' of the church takes on much of the responsibility for the spiritual growth and development of the child.

Anointing a baby with oil and marking the sign of the cross on its forehead is an important part of baptism.

For your Information

During the Anglican service of infant baptism three questions are directed at parents and god-parents. They are:

Priest: Do you turn to Christ?
Answer: I turn to Christ.
Priest: Do you repent of your sins?
Answer: I repent of my sins.
Priest: Do you renounce evil?
Answer: I renounce evil.

The same questions are also asked much later if a person comes forward to offer himself or herself for confirmation. On that occasion, however, the person is able to answer the questions for him or herself.

Key Points

1 The Roman Catholic, Anglican and Orthodox Churches are strongly committed to infant baptism, although there is no suggestion in the New Testament that it was ever practised by the early Christians.
2 In the Orthodox Church baptism and confirmation are combined in the single service of chrismation.
3 Baptism is essentially linked with cleansing from sin and the beginning of Church membership.

Work to do

1 The photograph on page 118 shows a font in a church. This plays an important part in the service of infant baptism. Can you find out:
   a Where the font is always traditionally to be found in a church – and why?
   b Where the font is often placed in modern churches – and why?
   c What this change implies for our understanding of infant baptism?
2 a What is happening in the photograph above?
   b What does this symbolic act mean?
3 'All Christians should have their babies baptised, but those who are not believers should not do so.'
   a Do you agree with the first part of this statement? Explain your answer, giving your reasons.
   b Several vicars have refused to baptise babies because their parents do not attend church. Do you think that this is a fair attitude for them to take?

In the Glossary

Anglican Church • Baptism • Chrismation • Circumcision • Confirmation • Font • Holy Spirit • Infant baptism • John the Baptist • New Testament • Orthodox Church • Priest • Roman Catholic Church

9.5 Believer's baptism

What is the service of believer's baptism, and what does it symbolise for those taking part?

A small and persecuted group of Anglican Christians in the 16th century, called Anabaptists, left Britain for Holland, insisting that the only people who could be baptised were adults who had committed their lives to Christ. They believed that other forms of baptism were worthless. Even those baptised as babies needed to be re-baptised as adults if the teaching of the Bible was to be followed. The Anabaptists were the forerunners of the modern Baptist Church, which now has 200,000 members in Great Britain and over 25 million in the USA. Whilst a few other Churches, such as the Brethren, also offer believer's baptism, it is usually only secondary to infant baptism. The Baptist Church is the only major Church which is fully committed to adult believer's baptism alone.

What is believer's baptism?

Baptists argue strongly that the only form of baptism known in the New Testament is that of believer's baptism. They point out that Jesus was baptised by John the Baptist when he was an adult, and that John's baptism was not offered to children. This is reinforced by Peter, in his sermon on the day of Pentecost, who told converts:

> "Each one of you must turn away from his sins and be baptised in the name of Jesus Christ, so that your sins will be forgiven; and you will receive God's gift, the Holy Spirit."
> (Acts 2.38)

Many Christians try to follow the example of Jesus and the apostles as closely as they can by being baptised in a sea, lake or river – if not the River Jordan itself. It was certainly the tradition in the early years of Christianity that a baptism should always be performed in running water. The majority nowadays, though, are baptised in their local Baptist church where a special pool (the baptistery) is sunk into the floor at the front for this purpose. Although baptisms in the early Church were only carried out at Easter or Pentecost they can now be performed at any

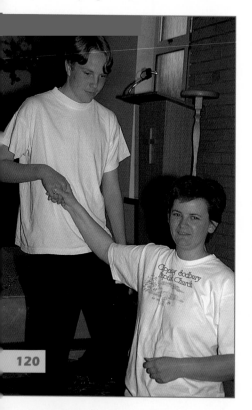

Going down into the pool is linked with dying with Jesus.

Being beneath the water is linked with burial with Jesus.

Coming up out of the water is linked with rising with Christ.

time of the year. The old custom of those being baptised wearing white – the colour of purity and forgiveness – largely remains, with most women wearing a simple white dress and men a white shirt and grey trousers for the service.

The service of believer's baptism is carried out in front of the whole church, and starts with each individual making a personal statement of their own Christian faith. Three important symbolic acts then take place which make believer's baptism very different from infant baptism:

1 The person goes down some steps into the pool. This indicates that they intend to leave their old life behind them. They are said to be dying to that old life – just as Jesus died on the cross.

2 For a brief moment the minister rocks the person back in the water so that their whole body is beneath the surface. This symbolises the death of all that the old life represents, and the 'burial' of the person with Christ who spent three days in the tomb.

3 The person comes up out of the water. Some pools have a different set of steps for the person to leave by, to show that the new life that they are now sharing with Jesus has already begun. Christ rose from the dead after three days and they are 'rising' to new life as well.

There is obviously a very close similarity between what happened to Jesus in the River Jordan (see Unit 9.3) and the service of believer's baptism. For the Christian the service points to changes in his or her life which have, or will, take place. One of those changes is for the baptised believer to become a full and active member of the Church. This starts at the first Lord's Supper after baptism, when the person is given the 'right hand of fellowship' by the minister (a handshake) and welcomed as a full Church member by the congregation. He or she is now expected to play a full part in the Church's work in the community by proclaiming the Christian message to those outside the Church. In the Baptist, and other Free Churches, this work of proclaiming the Christian message to the outside world is called 'evangelism'.

Key Points

1 Just as Jesus was baptised in the River Jordan so many Christians, especially Baptists, carry out Believer's baptism.
2 In Believer's baptism a person expresses their own faith in Jesus who has forgiven their sins.
3 Believer's baptism is a necessary stage before a person can become a full member of a Baptist church.

Work to do

1 a What is believer's baptism?
   b Describe two ways in which believer's baptism resembles the baptism of Jesus, and two ways in which it may be different.
   c 'Christians should follow the example of Jesus and only be baptised when they are adult.' Do you agree with this? Give some reasons to support your answer.
2 The ceremony of believer's baptism is full of symbolism. Explain the symbolic significance of:
   a the waters of baptism;
   b going down into the pool to be baptised;
   c being beneath the waters;
   d coming up out of the waters.
   Why do you think that such a high degree of importance is placed on the symbolic meaning of the service?
3 Describe the ceremony of believer's baptism.
4 Why do you think that it is important for many Christians to follow the example of Jesus as closely as possible when they are baptised? What might this involve?

In the Glossary

Apostle • Baptism • Baptist Church • Believer's baptism • Bible • Easter • Holy Spirit • John the Baptist • Lord's Supper • New Testament • Pentecost • Peter

Here is a list of the important events, parables, miracles and teachings of Jesus to help you to find you way around this book.

Events

The preaching of John the Baptist (1.1–8)

The baptism and temptations of Jesus (1.9–13)

The call of the four fishermen (1.14–20)

Jesus chooses his 12 disciples (3.13–19)

Jesus sends out his disciples (6.6–13)

The death of John the Baptist (6.14–29)

Peter's declaration at Caesarea Philippi (8.27–30)

The Transfiguration (9.2–13)

Jesus blesses the little children (10.13–16)

The rich man and Jesus (10.17–31)

Jesus enters Jerusalem (11.1–11)

Jesus clears the Temple (11.15–18)

The widow's offering (12.41–44)

Jesus is anointed at Bethany (14.3–9)

Jesus eats the Passover meal with his disciples (14.12–21)

The Lord's Supper (14.22–25)

Gethsemane (14.32–42)

The arrest of Jesus (14.43–52)

Jesus before the Sanhedrin (14.53–65)

The denial of Peter (14.66–72)

The trial before Pilate (15.1–20)

Jesus is crucified (15.21–32)

The death of Jesus (15.33–41)

The burial of Jesus (15.42–47)

The resurrection of Jesus (16.1–8)

The parables

New cloth on an old coat (2.21)

New wine in old wineskins (2.22)

The sower and the soils (4.3–8, 14–20)

The lamp under a bowl (4.21–22)

The growing seed (4.26–29)

The mustard seed (4.30–32)

The tenants in the vineyard (12.1–11)

The fig-tree (13.28–29)

The watchful servants (13.35–37)

The miracles

The healing miracles

The possessed man in synagogue (1.23–28)

Peter's mother-in-law (1.30–31)

The man with leprosy (1.40–42)

The paralysed man (2.3–12)

The man with a withered hand (3.1–5)

The two men from Gadara (5.1–15)

The woman with a haemorrhage (5.25–34)

The Canaanite woman's daughter (7.24–30)

The deaf mute (7.31–37)

The blind man at Bethsaida (8.22–26)

The boy with a demon (9.17–29)

The blind Bartimaeus (10.46–52)

Command over the forces of nature

Calming the storm (4.37–41)

Feeding 5,000 people (6.31–44)

Walking on the water (6.45–51)

Feeding 4,000 people (8.1–9)

The fig-tree withered (11.12–14, 20–25)

Bringing the dead back to life

Jairus' daughter (5.22–24, 35–43)

The resurrection of Jesus (16.1–8)

The teaching of Jesus

Fasting (2.18–22)

The Sabbath day (2.23–28)

Prophets in their home town (6.1–6)

The teaching of the ancestors (7.1–13)

The things that make a person unclean (7.14–23)

His own suffering and death (8.31–38, 9.30–32, 10.32–34)

Who is the greatest? (9.33–37)

Whoever is not for us is against us (9.38–41)

Temptations to sin (9.42–50)

Divorce (10.1–12)

Little children and God's kingdom (10.13–16)

Riches and God's kingdom (10.17–31)

Greatness (10.33–45)

The authority of Jesus (11.27–33)

Paying taxes (12.13–17)

Rising from the dead (12.18–27)

The Great Commandment (12.28–34)

The Messiah (12.35–37)

The destruction of the Temple (13.1–2)

Troubles and persecutions (13.3–13)

The end of time (13.14–23)

The coming of the Son of Man (13.24–27)

Be on guard (13.32–37)

The body of Jesus is laid in a tomb three days before he rises from the dead. The return of Jesus from the dead is the most important event in Mark's Gospel.

Advent From the Latin word meaning 'arrival', the first season of the Christian year, beginning on the last Sunday in November. It is a time of preparation for the coming of Jesus at Christmas.

Allegory A story similar to a parable, but one in which each of its many parts has a symbolic meaning.

Altar From the Latin word meaning 'high', the holy table in most churches where the bread and wine for Holy Communion are blessed and offered to God.

Andrew The brother of Simon Peter, and one of the disciples of Jesus, who was martyred in 60 CE.

Angel A supernatural being sent to bring special revelations from God to human beings. Good (Angel Gabriel) and bad (Satan) angels are recognised in Mark's Gospel.

Anglican Church The worldwide fellowship of different Churches which are based on the teachings of the Church of England. All of the Anglican Churches accept the leadership of the Archbishop of Canterbury.

Apostle A word, meaning 'to send', applied to the disciples of Jesus after the resurrection. It then came to indicate any follower of Jesus.

Baptism The sacrament by which people become members of the Christian Church. In the Roman Catholic, Anglican and Orthodox Churches, baptism is carried out on babies (infant baptism), but in Baptist churches it is performed on adults (believer's baptism).

Baptist Church One of the largest worldwide Protestant denominations. Begun in 1609, the Baptist Church is committed to baptising adults when they profess to have faith in Jesus as their Saviour.

Believer's baptism The practice in Baptist Churches, and a few others, of baptising only adults who have faith in Jesus Christ.

Bible The sacred book for all Christians. It is in two parts – the Old Testament and the New Testament.

Bishop A senior priest, an office traced by some Churches back to the twelve Apostles. Bishops are the only priests able to ordain and conduct confirmations.

Blasphemy Any speech or thought that shows a contempt for God.

Breaking of Bread One of the favourite Protestant terms for describing the service of Holy Communion. The service reminds believers of the early Church where people met together to 'break bread' – to eat a simple meal which also became a celebration of faith.

Chrismation After a baby is baptised in the Orthodox Church, he or she is anointed by a priest to receive the Holy Spirit. It is the same as confirmation in other Churches.

Christ The Greek form of the Hebrew word for 'Messiah', meaning 'Anointed One'.

Church of England The Church formed in the 16th century by King Henry VIII after a quarrel with the Pope. It became the established (official) Church in England under Elizabeth I.

Circumcision The cutting away of the foreskin on a Jewish boy's penis when he is eight days old. It is the oldest Jewish custom, which is still continued today.

Communion table The table at the front of a Free Church, from behind which the service of the Lord's Supper is conducted.

Confirmation The service performed in Roman Catholic and Anglican Churches, in which a person 'confirms' the promises made by others for them when they were baptised. This service can only be performed by a bishop.

Day of Pentecost The festival of Pentecost at which the Holy Spirit was given to the first Christians.

Devil See Satan.

Disciple The term used to describe the followers of Jesus; literally 'someone who learns' or 'is a pupil'.

Easter The festival celebrating the death and resurrection of Jesus, which runs from Good Friday to Easter Sunday. The name was taken over by the early Christians from the Old English word 'eostre', which was a pagan festival.

Elijah The most important of the Old Testament prophets, who lived in Israel in the 9th century BCE.

Epistle A letter. There are many epistles in the New Testament written by Paul, Peter, John and others.

Eucharist The favourite term used for the service of Holy Communion in the Anglican Church; it literally means 'Thanksgiving'.

Exodus The journey of the Israelites (Jews) out of Egyptian slavery under Moses towards the Promised Land. This was the greatest event in Jewish history.

Exorcism The driving out of a spirit or a demon from someone who is possessed by it.

Fasting An activity common amongst some Christians, which involves going without food and drink to devote oneself to spiritual affairs.

Font The stone container used to hold water for infant baptism; it literally means 'spring of water'.

Free Churches The Churches, such as Baptist and Methodist, which do not owe allegiance to Anglican or Roman Catholic Churches.

Gentile A person who is not a Jew.

Good Friday The day, two days before Easter Sunday, when Christians remember the death of Jesus.

Gospel One of the four books in the New Testament which describe the life and teaching of Jesus – Matthew, Mark, Luke and John.

Herod Antipas The son of Herod the Great, who ruled over Galilee after his father's death.

Herod the Great The King of Judea between 39 and 5 BCE. Herod rebuilt the Jewish Temple in Jerusalem, and tried to kill the baby Jesus by slaughtering all of the baby boys under the age of two.

Herodians The group dedicated to keeping the descendants of Herod the Great on the throne.

High Priest The leader of the Jewish community in the time of Jesus. The High Priest wore a special breastplate, and was the only person able to enter the Holy of Holies in the Temple where God was believed to dwell.

Holy Communion The Christian service otherwise known as the Eucharist, the Mass or the Holy Liturgy, which commemorates the death of Jesus. At Holy Communion, worshippers eat bread and drink wine.

Holy Liturgy The most important service in the Orthodox Church, similar to Holy Communion in other Churches.

Holy Spirit The third member of the Christian Trinity, together with God the Father and God the Son. The Holy Spirit is also known as the Holy Ghost.

Holy Unction The Roman Catholic service at which the priest anoints with oil those who are approaching death.

Holy Week The week in the Christian year which starts with Palm Sunday and ends on Easter Sunday.

Icon A painting of Jesus, or of one of the saints, used mainly in Orthodox worship.

Iconostasis The screen in Orthodox churches which separates the sanctuary containing the High Altar from the nave where the people sit.

Infant baptism The service in Anglican, Roman Catholic and Orthodox Churches in which a baby is anointed with water. Infant baptism is the admission to Church membership.

James The brother of John, and one of the inner circle of Jesus' disciples along with Peter and John.

Jerusalem The city which is central to Judaism, Christianity and Islam. It was first captured by King David, it was the place where Solomon first built the Temple, and it was the city in which Jesus was executed.

John Son of Zebedee, one of the disciples of Jesus. John probably wrote several books in the New Testament, including the fourth Gospel.

John the Baptist The cousin of Jesus, born to Elizabeth and Zechariah when they were very old. The preaching and baptising of John prepared the people for the coming of Jesus; John baptised Jesus himself in the River Jordan.

Judas Iscariot One of the original twelve disciples of Jesus, and the treasurer for the group, who betrayed Jesus to the Jewish authorities. He later committed suicide.

Kingdom of God The rule of God in the heart and the future rule of God in heaven. It is a phrase that often occurs in the teaching of Jesus, and is the theme of many of his parables.

Last Supper The final meal that Jesus ate with his disciples before he was arrested. He followed it by washing their feet.

Lent An important season in the Church year, which runs from Ash Wednesday through to Holy Saturday. It is a time of preparation for Easter.

Liturgy A service of worship which follows a prescribed ritual.

Lord's Supper The term used in Free Churches for Holy Communion. It is also known as the Breaking of Bread.

Luke A doctor and companion of Paul on his missionary journeys. He is the likely author of the Gospel that carries his name.

Mark A native of Jerusalem who accompanied Paul and Barnabus on their first missionary journey. He wrote the second Gospel around 65 CE.

Mass The Roman Catholic term for the Eucharist.

Matthew A tax-gatherer working for the Romans, called by Jesus to be one of his disciples. He wrote the first Gospel in the New Testament around 85 CE.

Messiah The Hebrew form of the Greek word 'Christ', meaning 'Anointed One'. In the Old Testament the Jews were told to expect a leader from God, the Messiah, who would deliver them from their enemies.

Methodist Church One of the largest Free Churches, based on the teachings of the 18th-century Anglican clergyman John Wesley.

Monk A man who lives in a monastery and takes the three-fold vow of chastity, obedience and poverty.

Moses The leader and law-giver in ancient Israel. Moses led the Israelites out of Egyptian slavery to the verge of the Promised Land, and passed on the Ten Commandments from God on Mt Sinai.

New Testament The second part of the Bible, which contains the four Gospels, the Acts of the Apostles and many letters written by early Church leaders.

Nun A woman who lives in a convent and takes the three-fold vow of chastity, obedience and poverty.

Old Testament The Christian title for the books of the Jewish Scriptures, divided into three parts – the Law (Torah), the Writings and the Prophets.

Ordination The service through which a man or a woman becomes a priest. Ordination confers the authority to give the sacraments.

Orthodox Church A family of different national Churches, mainly found in eastern Europe and the Middle East; it broke away from the Roman Catholic Church in 1054.

Palm Sunday The day at the start of Holy Week, on which Christians remember the entry of Jesus into Jerusalem on a donkey, to be welcomed by the people as their Messiah.

Parable A story told by Jesus, which was intended to teach a moral or a spiritual lesson.

Passover See Pesach.

Patriarch The title given in the different Orthodox Churches to their most senior bishops.

Paul A Pharisee who converted to Christianity on the Damascus road to become Christianity's first great missionary. Paul travelled throughout the Roman Empire and wrote many of the New Testament epistles, before being martyred in 64 CE.

Penance One of the seven sacraments of the Roman Catholic Church. In it a person seeks God's forgiveness and carries out a penalty (penance) to show sincerity.

Pentecost The Greek name for the Jewish Festival of Weeks, which takes place 50 days after Pesach.

Pesach The Hebrew name for the central Jewish festival of Passover, the yearly commemoration of the release of the Jews from Egyptian slavery.

Peter One of the disciples of Jesus, originally called Simon. Peter, a fisherman, plays a leading part in Mark's Gospel; he was the first Church leader after the resurrection of Jesus.

Pharisees The leading religious group at the time of Jesus. The aim of the Pharisees (literally 'the Separated Ones') was to obey and protect the teachings of the Torah.

Pontius Pilate The Roman procurator who condemned Jesus to death. Pilate was procurator of Judea from 26 to 36 CE.

Priest A man or woman who is authorised to lead services in Anglican, Roman Catholic and Orthodox churches. Priests are ordained by a bishop to give the sacraments.

Prophet A man or woman sent by God to carry a divine message.

Protestant A Christian who does not belong to the Roman Catholic or Orthodox Churches.

Quakers A Christian denomination started in the 17th century by George Fox, which places great emphasis on waiting for God ('the Inner Light') to speak in meetings.

Rabbi A Jewish teacher.

Reformation The religious revolution in Europe in the 16th-century Church, which led to the birth of Protestantism. The Reformation broke the power of the Roman Catholic Church in Britain.

Roman Catholic Church The worldwide community of Christians which follows the leadership of the Pope as the successor of St Peter on earth. It is the largest Christian denomination, with 1,000 million followers.

Royal Doors The doors through the iconostasis in an Orthodox church, leading to the High Altar. The Royal Doors are covered with icons.

Sabbath day The seventh day of the Jewish week (Friday evening to Saturday evening), set aside by God's command for rest and worship.

Sacrament An outward, physical sign of an inward, spiritual blessing; also, a service which communicates this blessing to worshippers.

Sadducees The priests of the Temple in the time of Jesus. They were disliked by their fellow-Jews because of their willingness to co-operate with the Romans.

Salvation Army An international Protestant organisation, started in the 19th century, which works mainly amongst poorer people in society. Its members wear a distinctive uniform.

Sanhedrin The Jewish Council, which condemned Jesus to death. The Sanhedrin had 71 members and met in Jerusalem.

Satan The supernatural being who is the main enemy of God. Satan, also known as the Devil, is presented in the New Testament as the leader of the rebellious angels and the source of all evil in world.

Scribe An expert in the Law of Moses, who was opposed to Jesus.

Second Coming The Christian belief that Jesus will return to the earth.

Sermon The part of a service where the priest or minister explains a passage from the Bible.

Shema 'Hear', the Jewish name for the words recorded in Deuteronomy 6.4 – the statement of belief which stands at the heart of the Jewish faith.

Son of Man The favourite description by Jesus of himself, which emphasises the human side of Jesus. It is often used in Mark's Gospel.

Stations of the Cross Fourteen sculptures or paintings in the Roman Catholic Church, which show important events leading up to death of Jesus.

Sunday 'The day of the sun', the first day of week. The day on which Jesus rose from the dead became the Christian holy day when Christianity and Judaism split from each other in the 1st century.

Synagogue The building in which a Jewish congregation meets for study, prayer and worship; the word literally means 'coming together'.

Synoptic Gospels The name given to the first three Gospels – Matthew, Mark and Luke – because they have a similar approach to the life of Jesus. The word 'synoptic' literally means 'seeing together'.

Temple A magnificent religious building in Jerusalem, first built by King Solomon in the 10th century BCE, and restored by Herod the Great in the time of Jesus.

Ten Commandments The ten laws given by God to the Jews on Mt Sinai. There is a summary of them in every synagogue.

Torah The first five books (and the most important part) of the Jewish Scriptures (Old Testament) – Genesis, Exodus, Leviticus, Deuteronomy and Numbers.

Transfiguration The event in which the appearance of Jesus was miraculously changed in front of his disciples Peter, James and John.

Transubstantiation The Roman Catholic belief that bread and wine at the Mass become the body and blood of Christ after consecration by the priest.

Trinity The central doctrine of the Christian faith, that there are three persons in the one God – God the Father, God the Son and God the Holy Spirit.

Via Dolorosa The road along which Jesus is believed to have walked on his way to crucifixion.

Vocation The belief that someone has been called by God to a special work – for example, to be a priest or a nun.

Zealots A group of Jews who were fanatically opposed to the Romans in the time of Jesus.